Mandolin Picking Tunes

CHRISTMAS IN THE BRITISH ISLES

by Tommy Norris

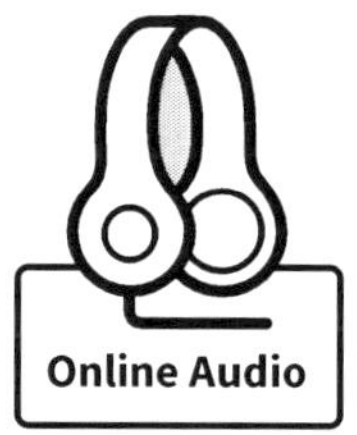

To access the online audio go to:
WWW.MELBAY.COM/30922MEB

The Northfield 'Big Mon' F-Style mandolin in Icelandic Brown finish on the cover is courtesy of Northfield Mandolins.

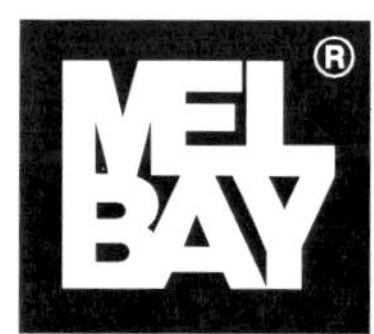

WWW.MELBAY.COM

Preface

Through the centuries, the joyous Christmas season has inspired musicians to compose countless hymns, carols, songs, and major orchestral and choral works. In the British Isles, the music created to celebrate this season has a flavor all its own that captures the beauty, mystery, and glory of Christmas.

In this book, Tommy Norris has arranged 20 Christmas melodies, including some very beautiful but lesser-known carols—with the goal of expanding the mandolin Christmas repertoire. I love the tunes he has selected. His solo arrangements embrace the essence of the tunes yet remain solidly *mandolinistic*!

All the solos are written in standard notation and tablature. Feel free to add your own left-hand fingering as needed. Tommy's recording of each solo is available as an online download. The URL for accessing these recordings can be found on the title page of this book.

I sincerely hope these fine arrangements add meaning and joy to your Christmas season.

William Bay

Index

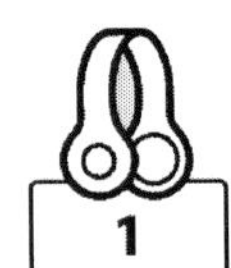

A Boy is Born in Bethlehem

13th Century English

Moderato ♩ = 124

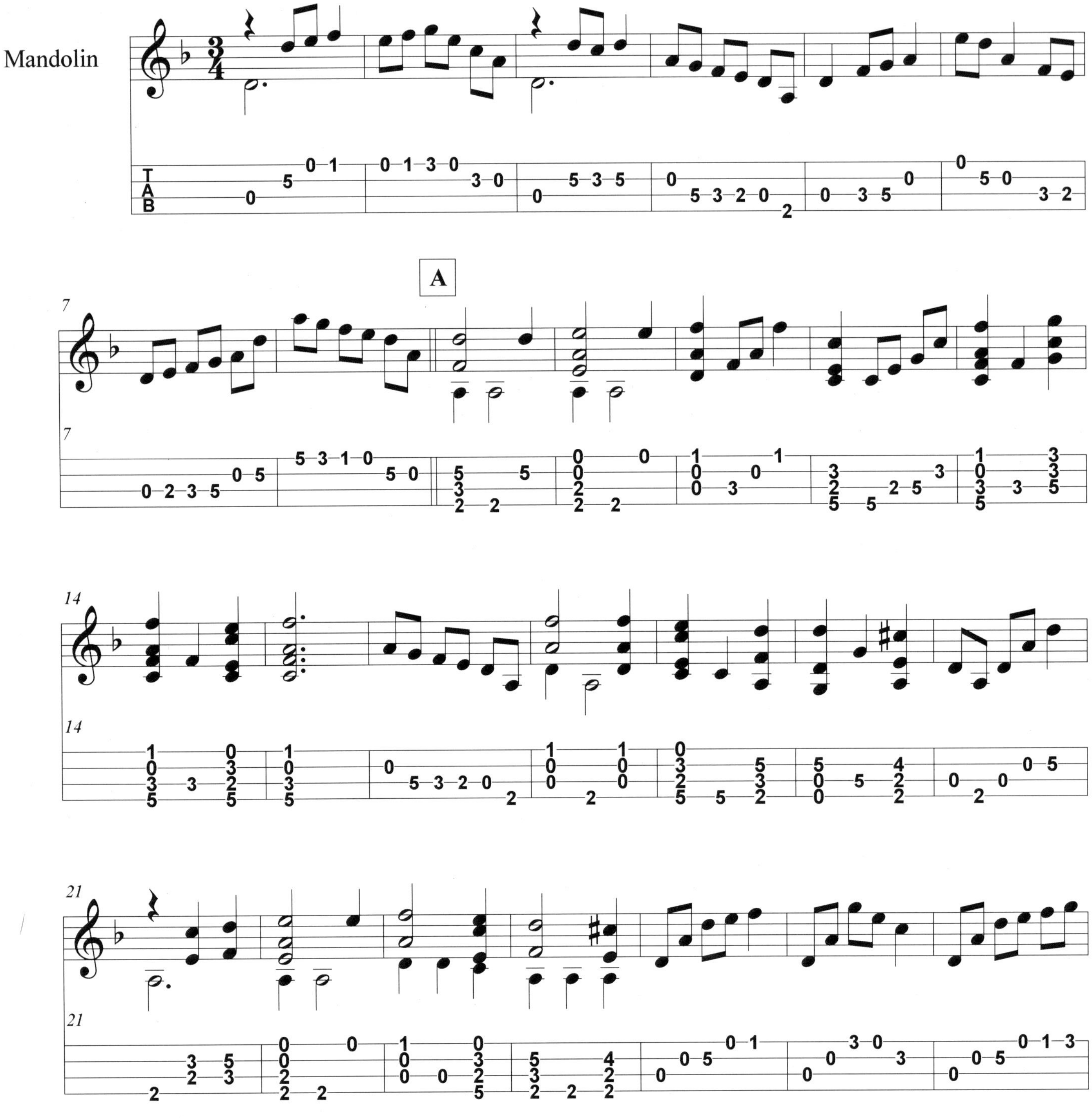

Mandolin

A

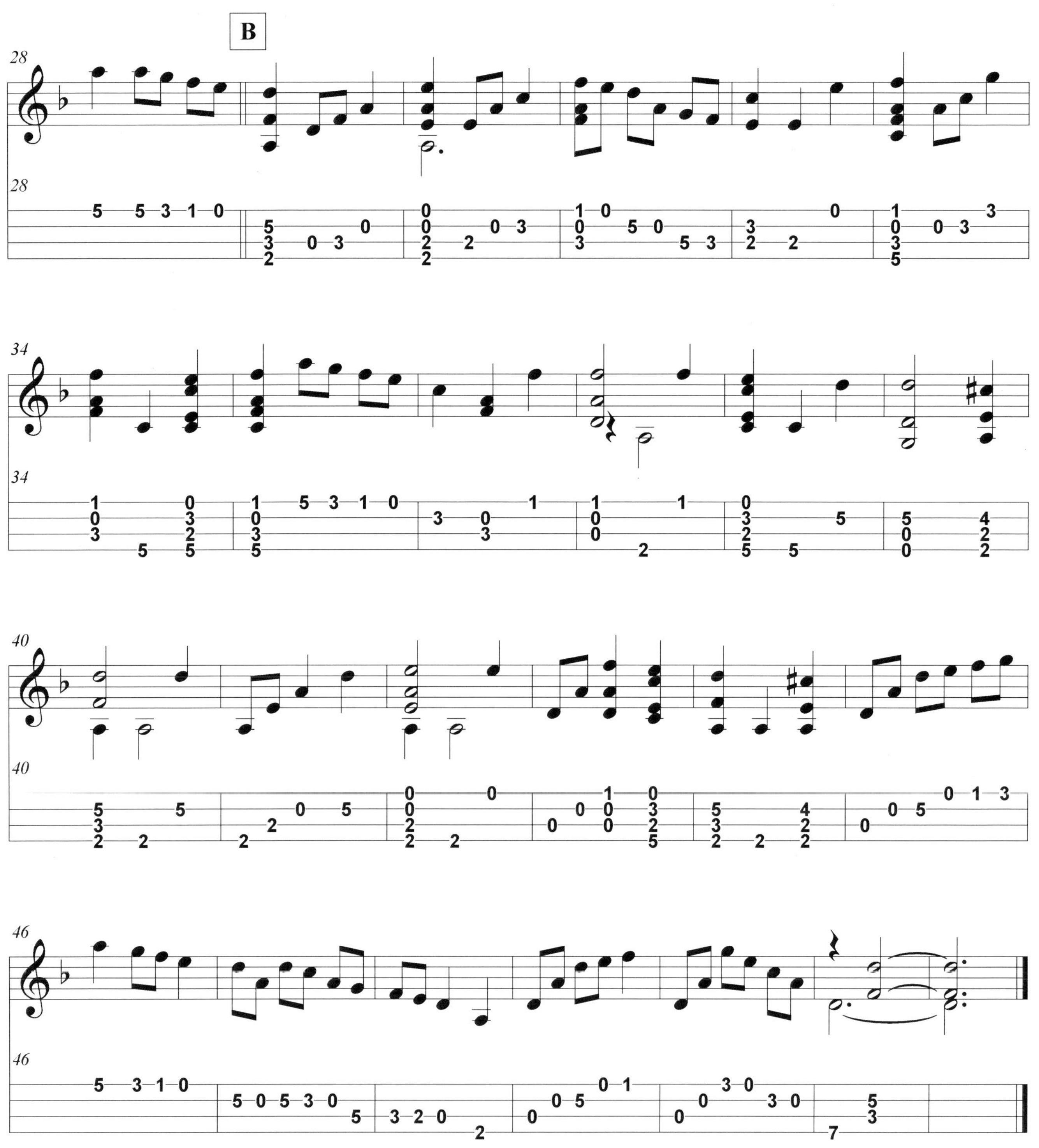
B

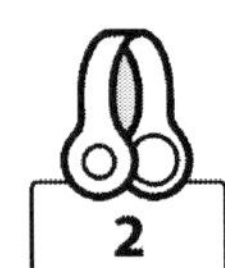

Away in a Manger

Cradle Song

William Kirkpatrick

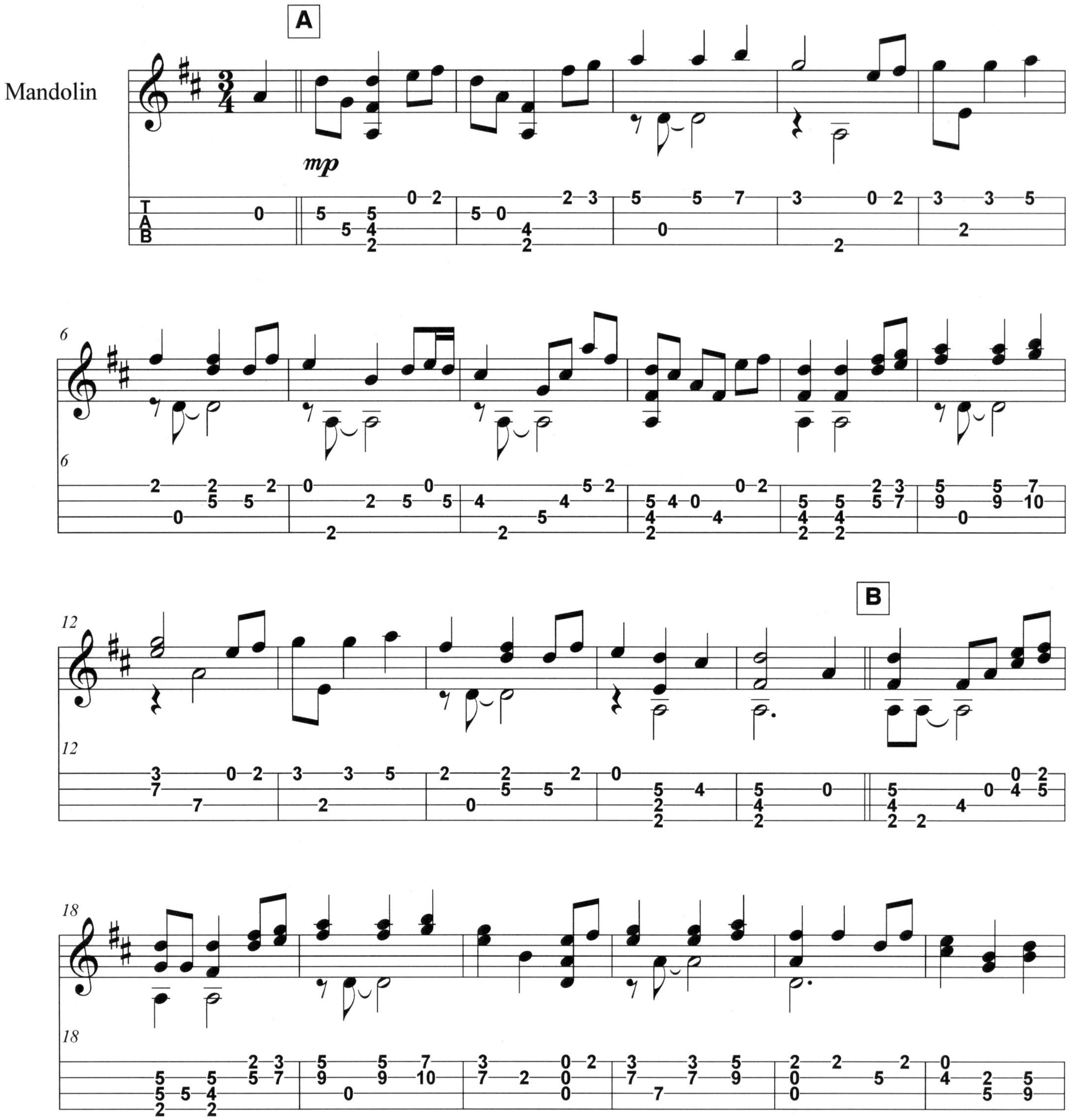

A

Mandolin

mp

B

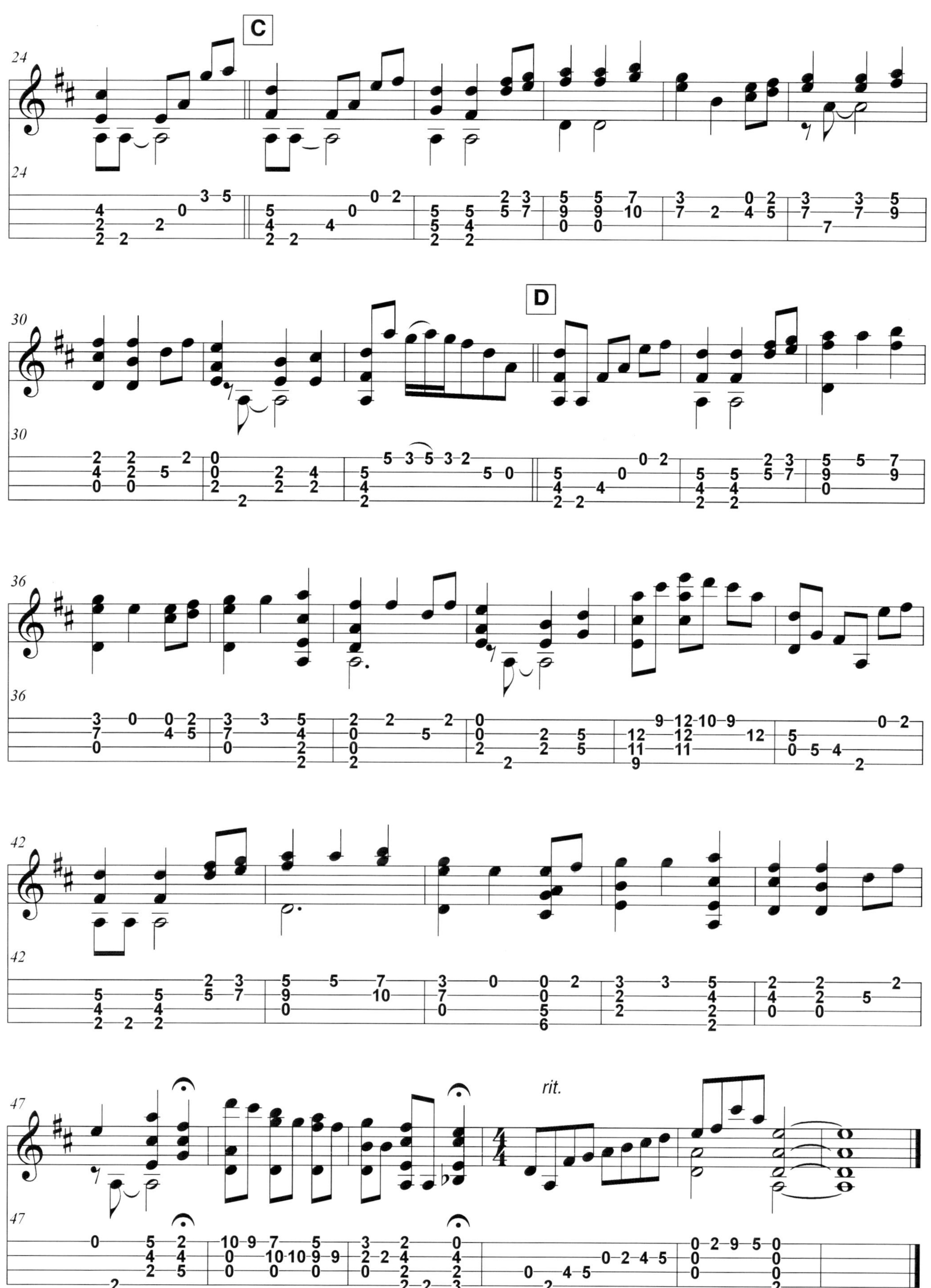

C
D
rit.

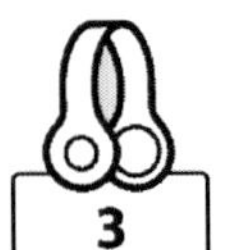

Baloo, Lammy

17th Century Scottish

Moderato ♩ = 120

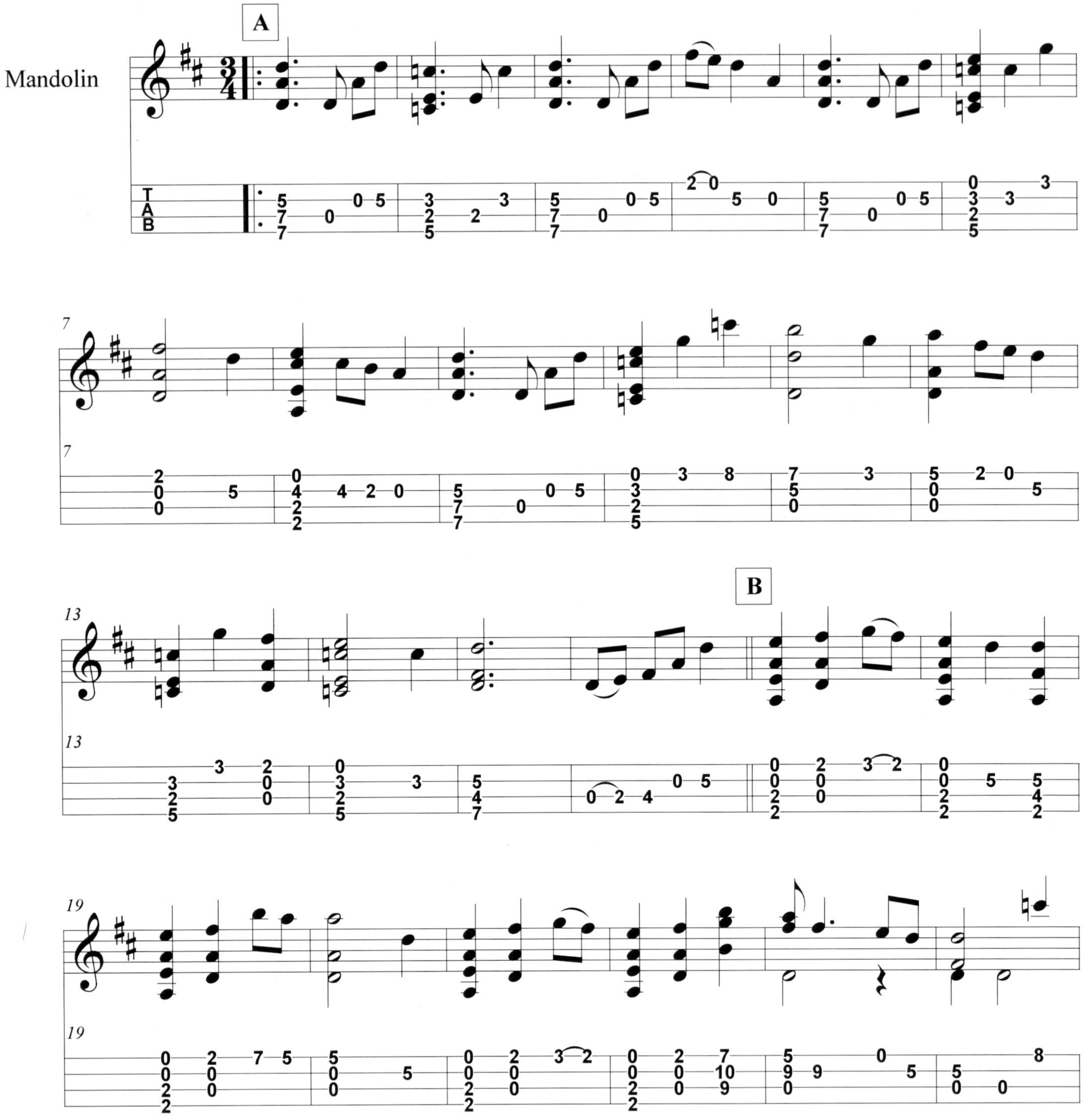

A

Mandolin

B

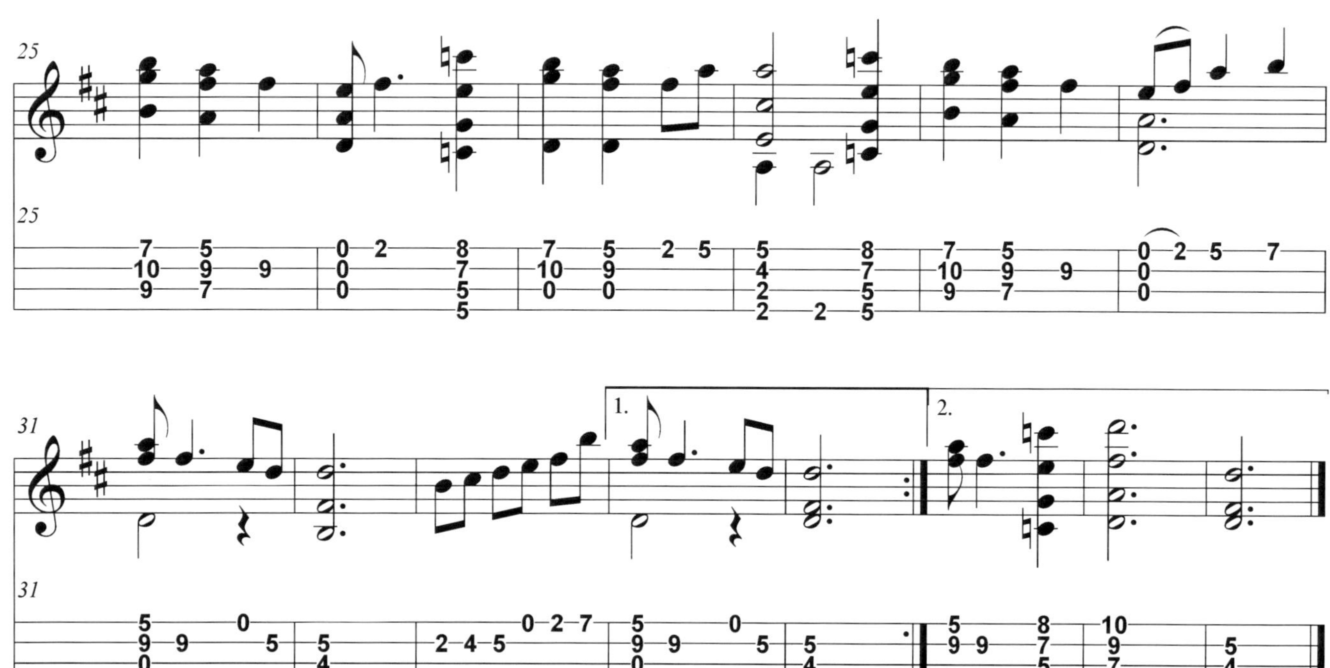

Blessed Be That Maid Marie

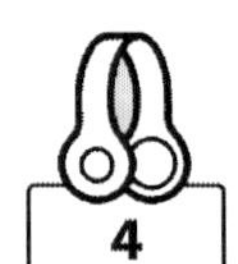

From William Ballet's Lute Book 1600

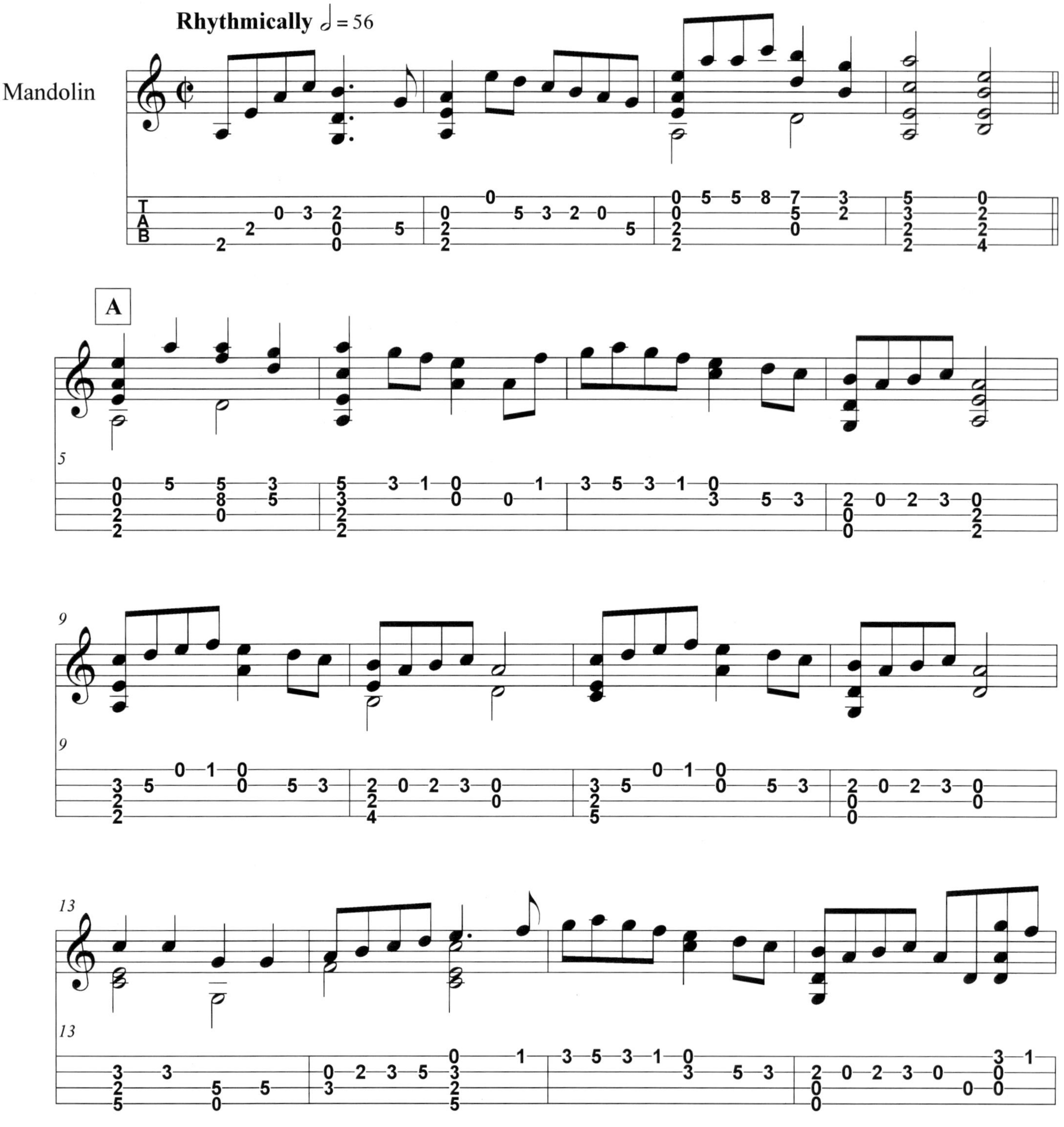

Rhythmically 𝅗𝅥 = 56

Mandolin

A

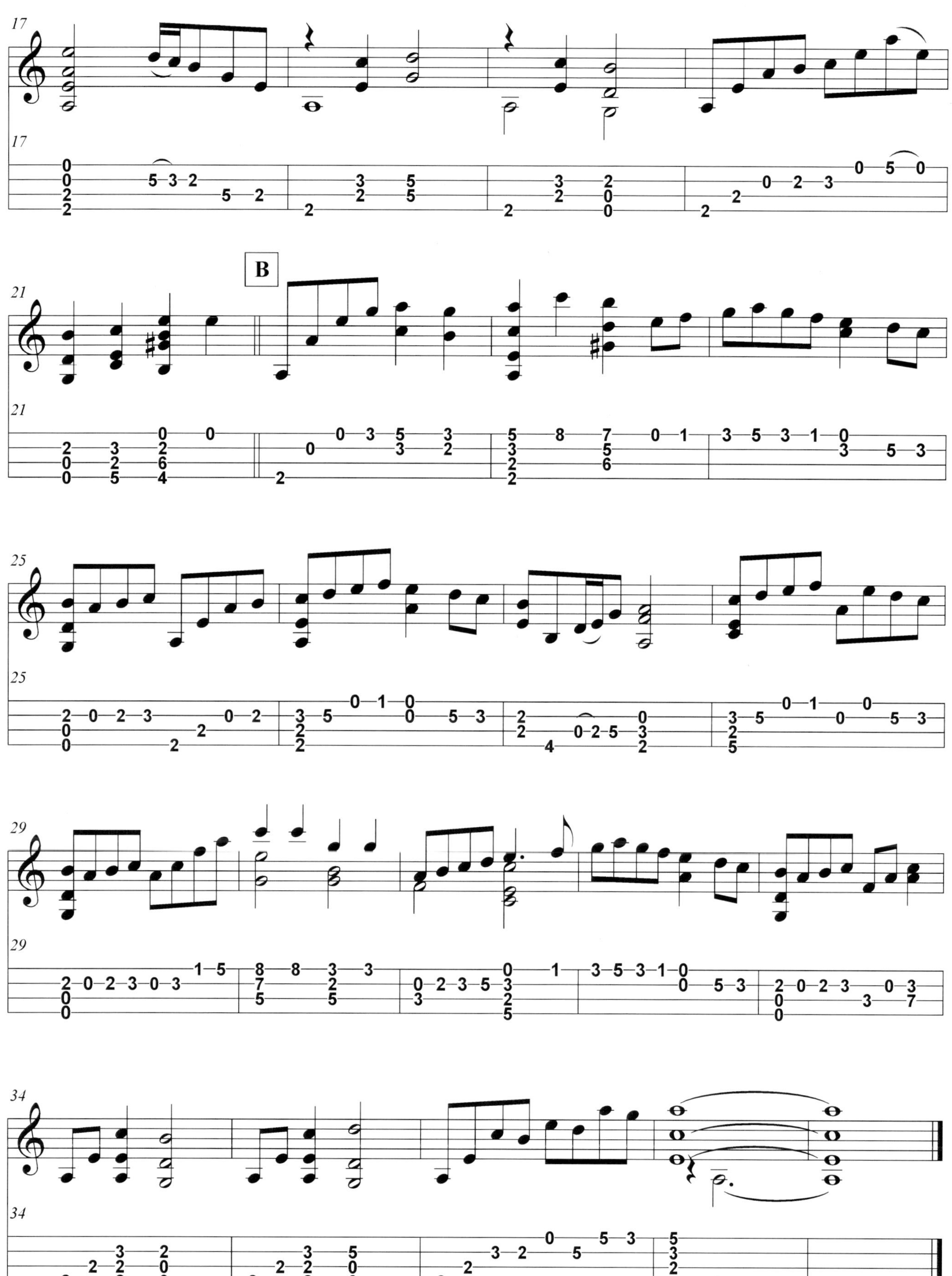
B

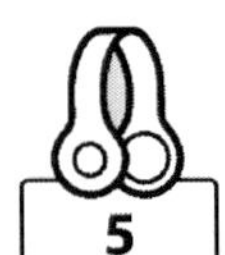

Carol of the Birds

Traditional English

Moderato ♩ = 100

A

Mandolin

B

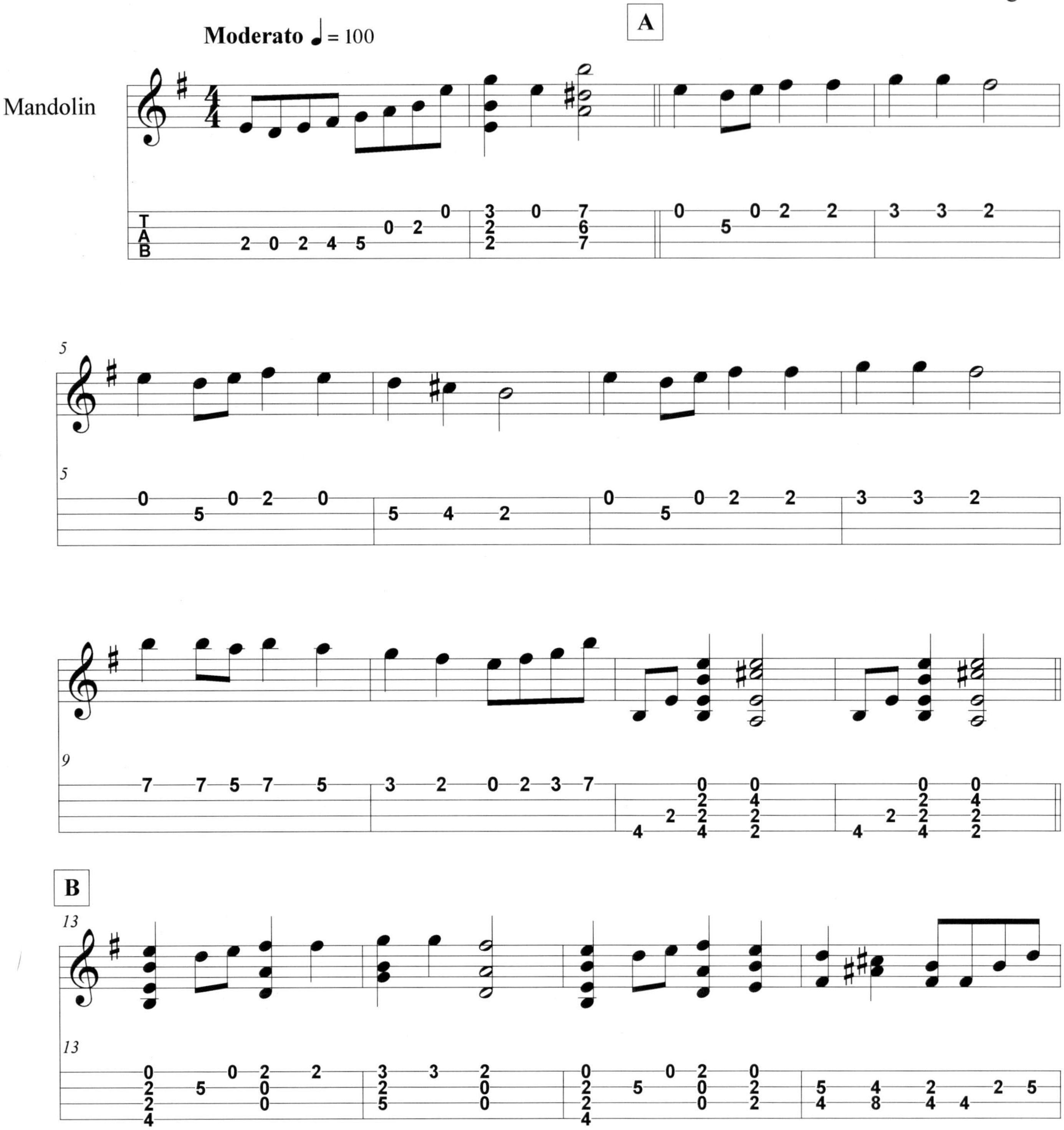

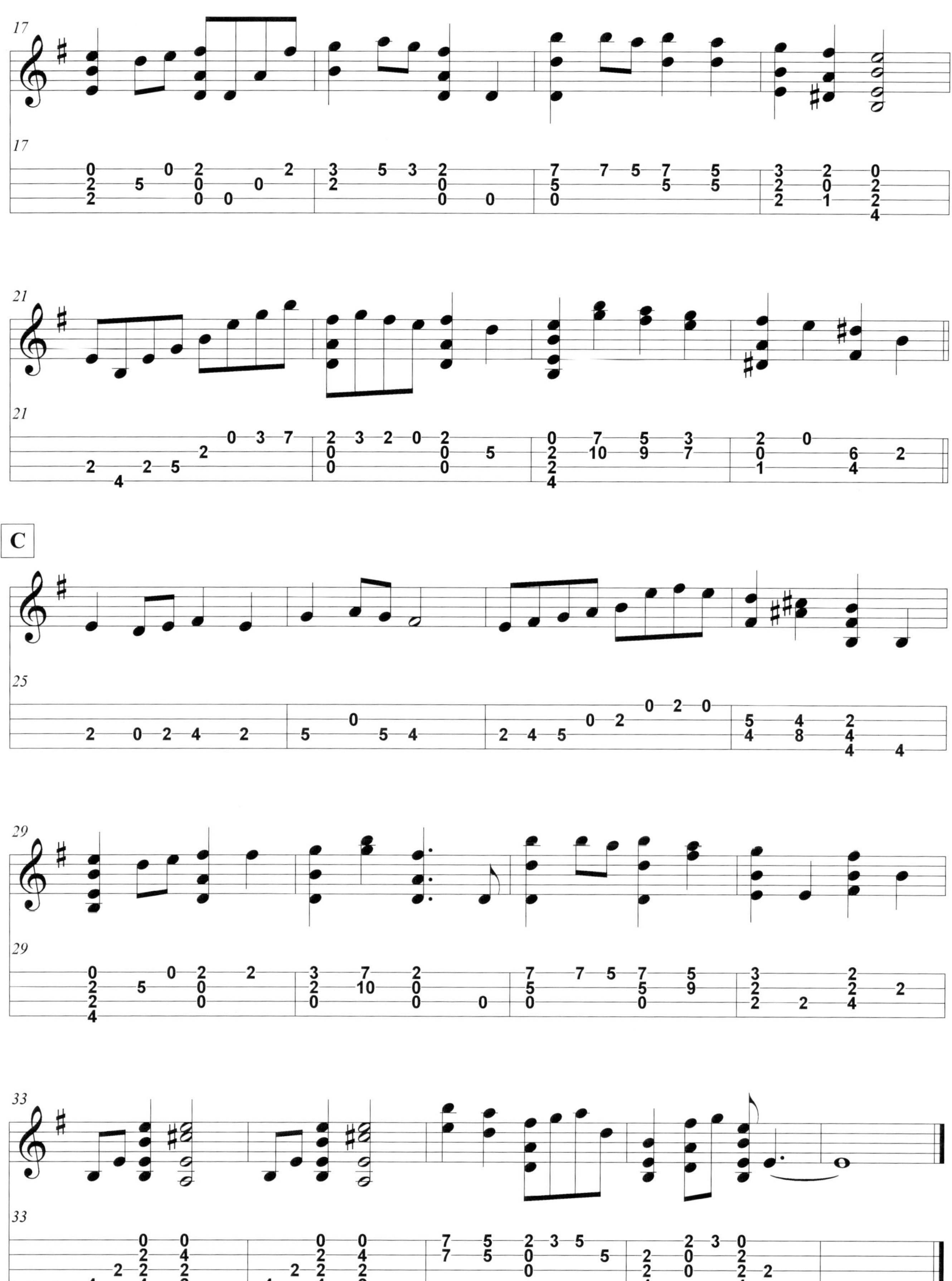
17
21
C
25
29
33

Coventry Carol

6

Traditional English

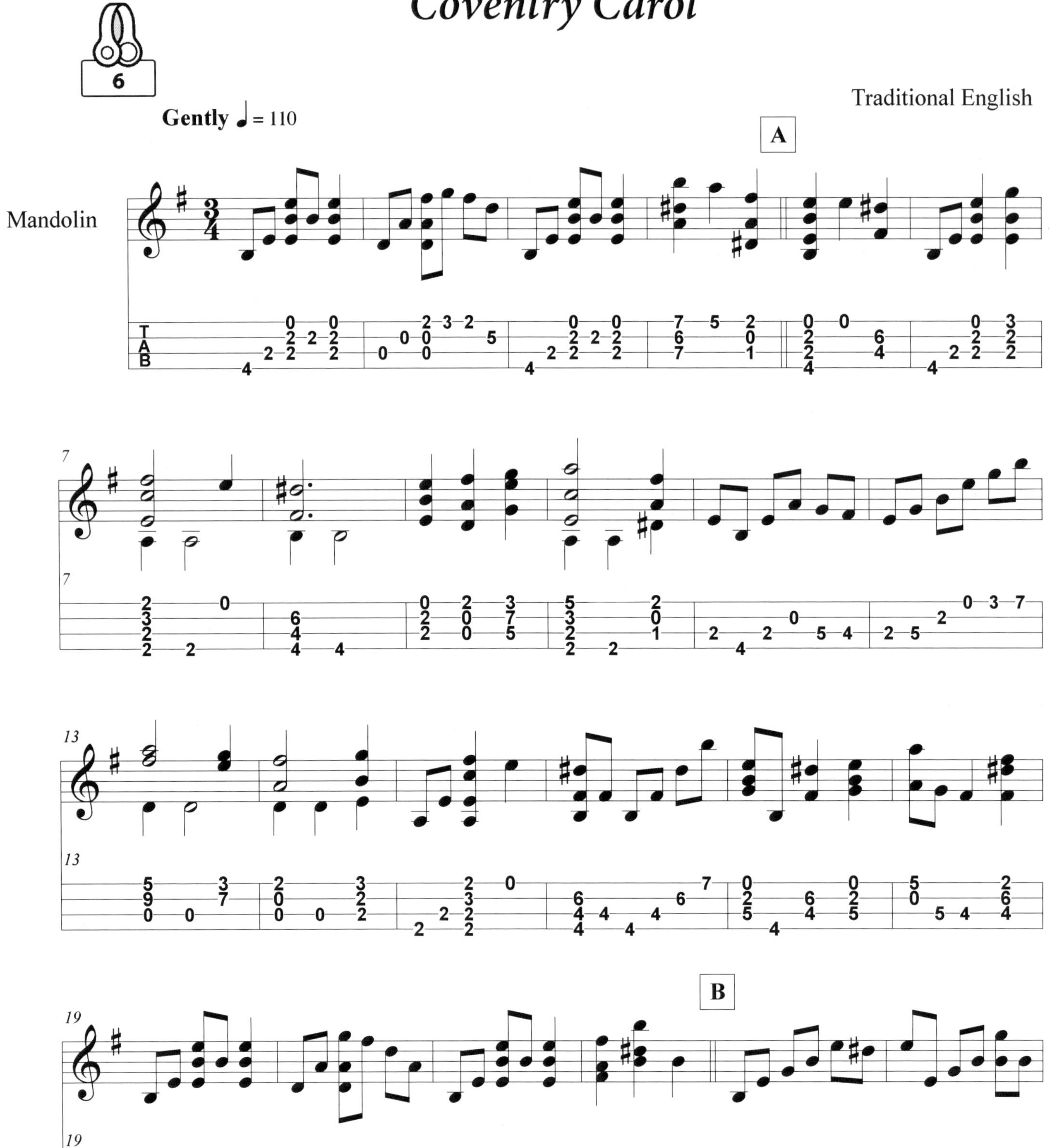

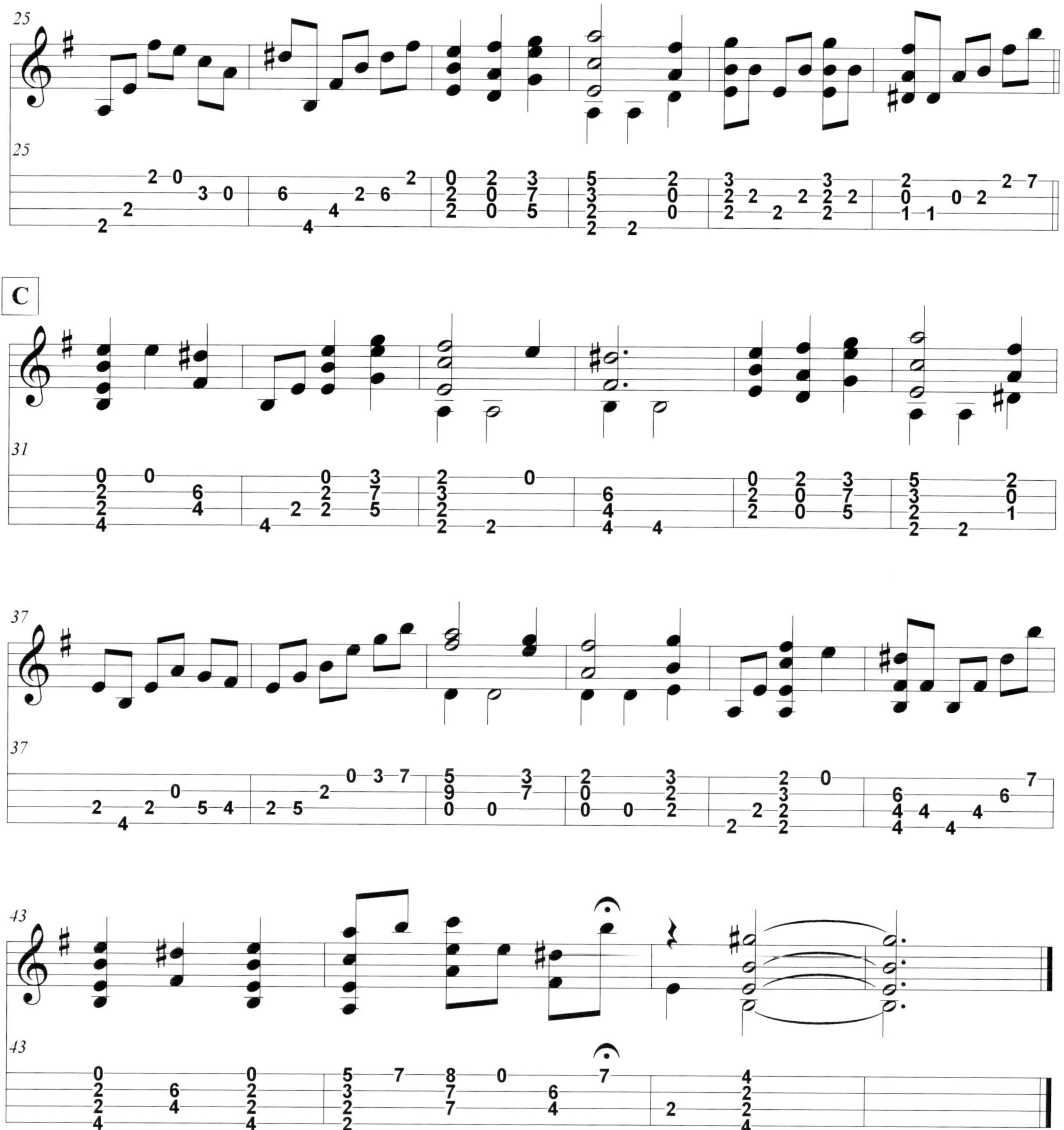
C

Ding Dong, Merrily on High

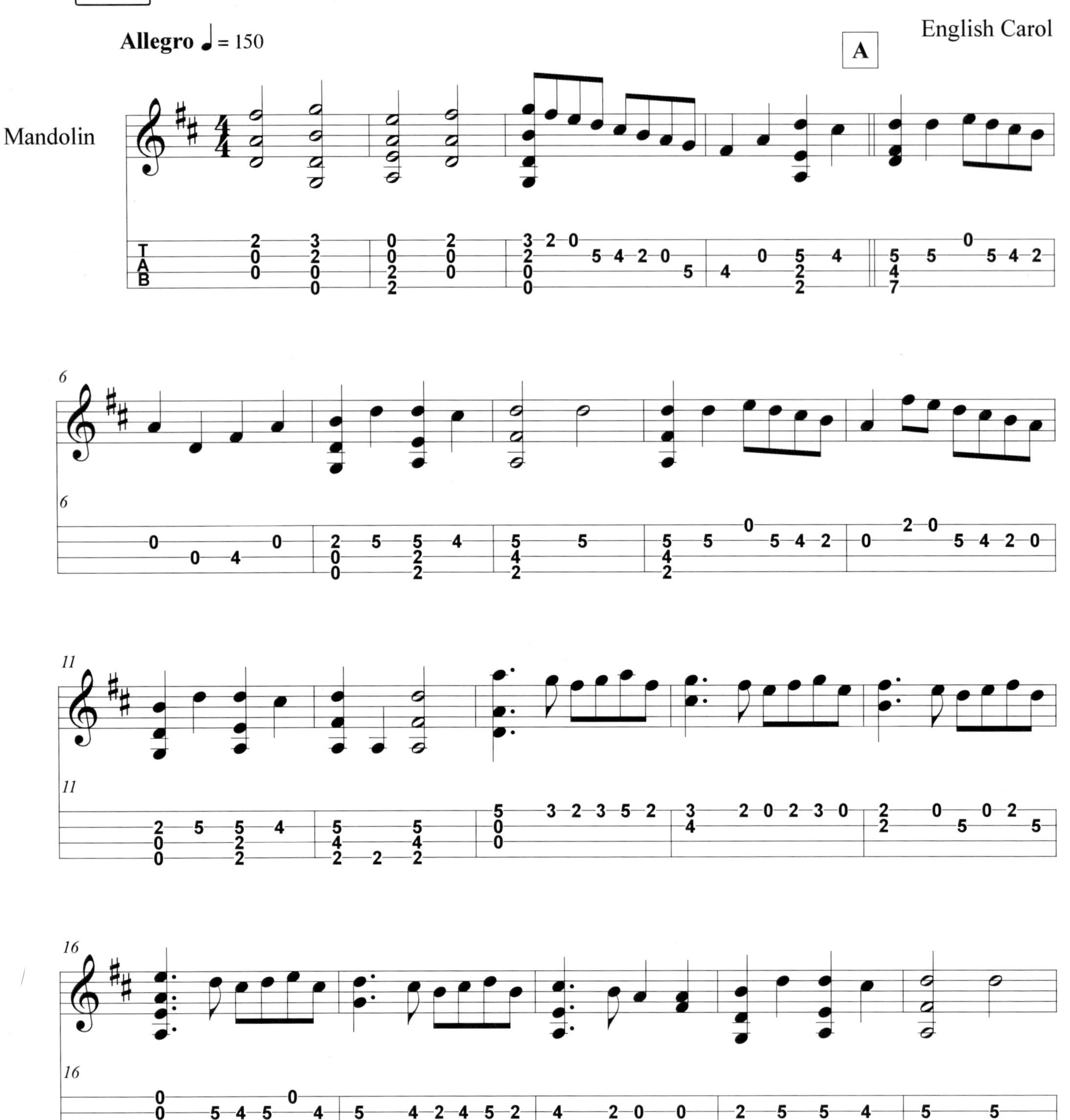

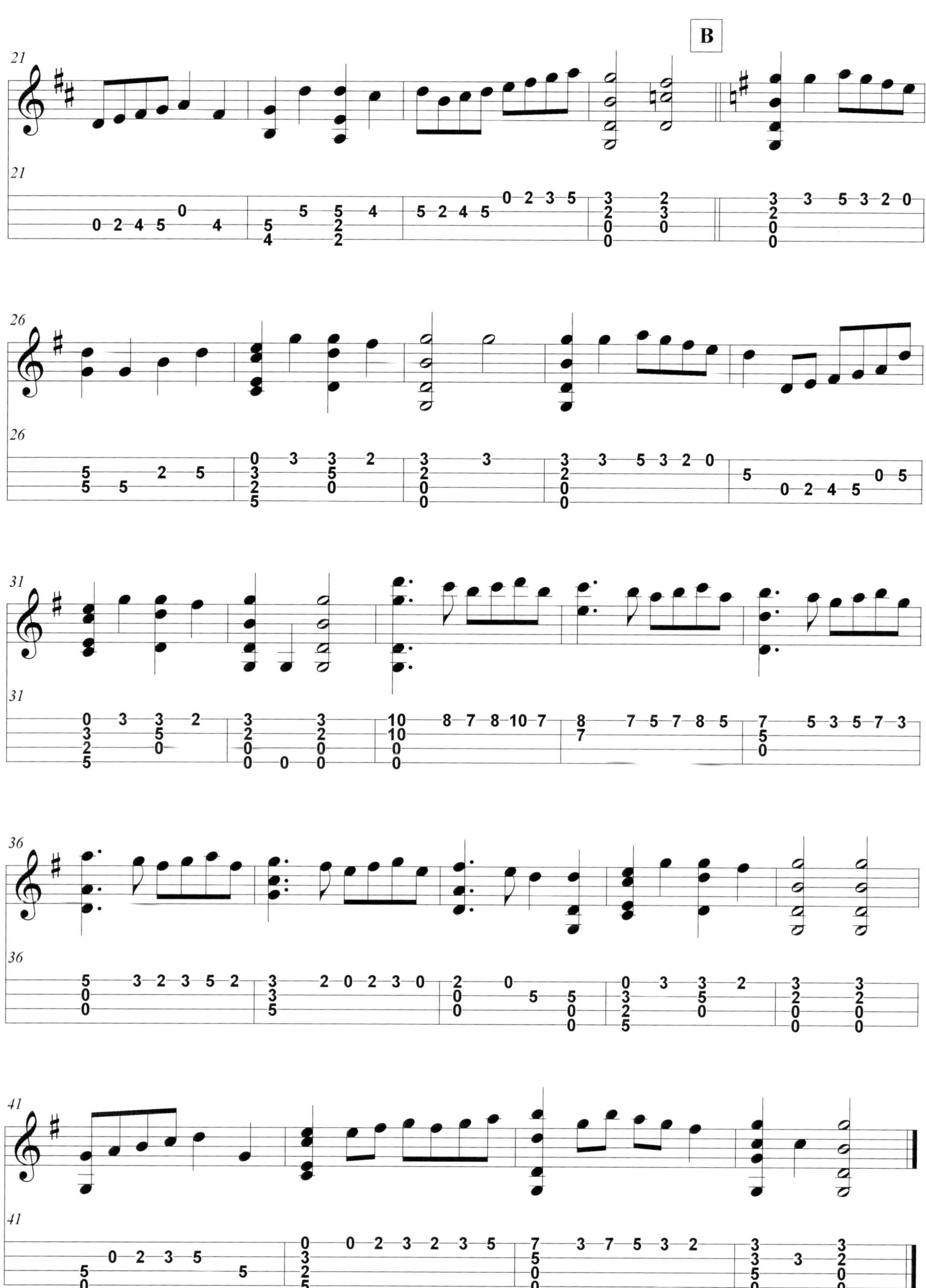
B
21
26
31
36
41

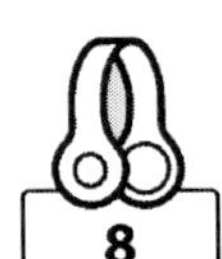

Down in Yon Forest

English Carol

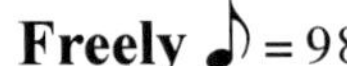

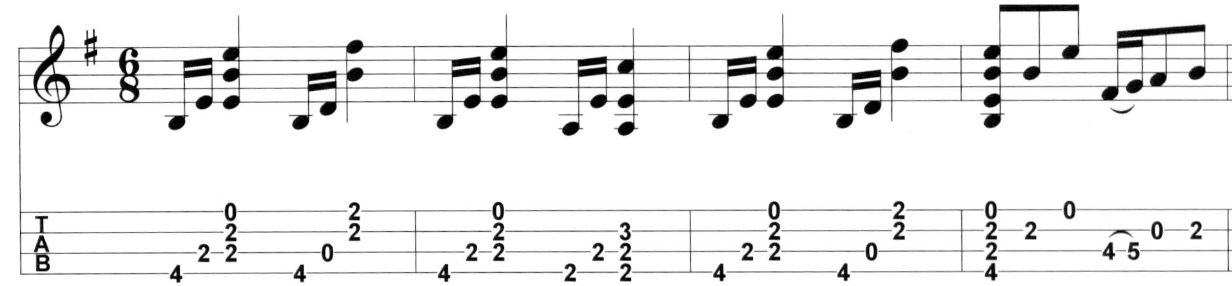

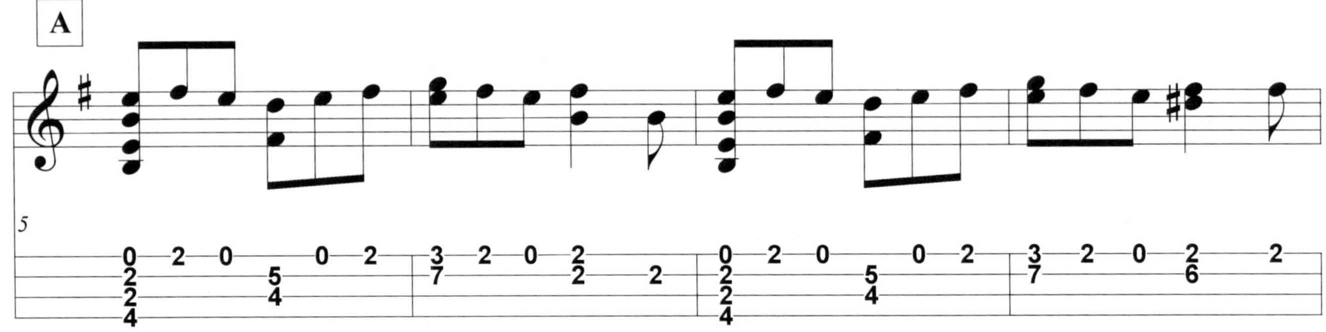

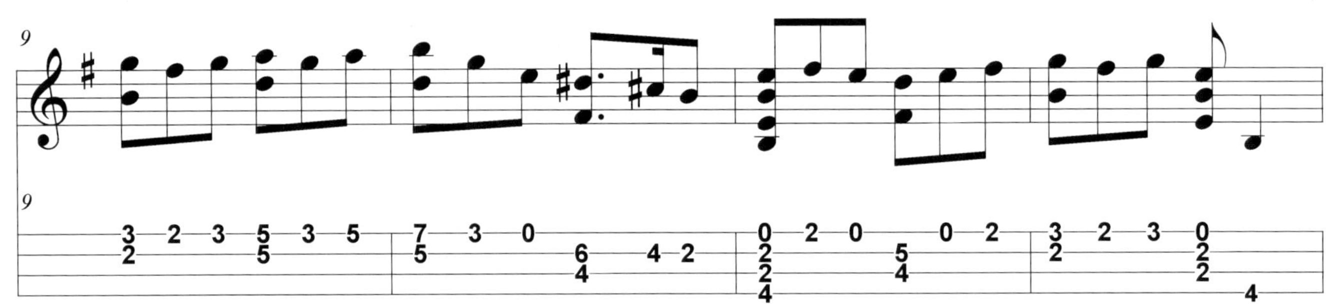

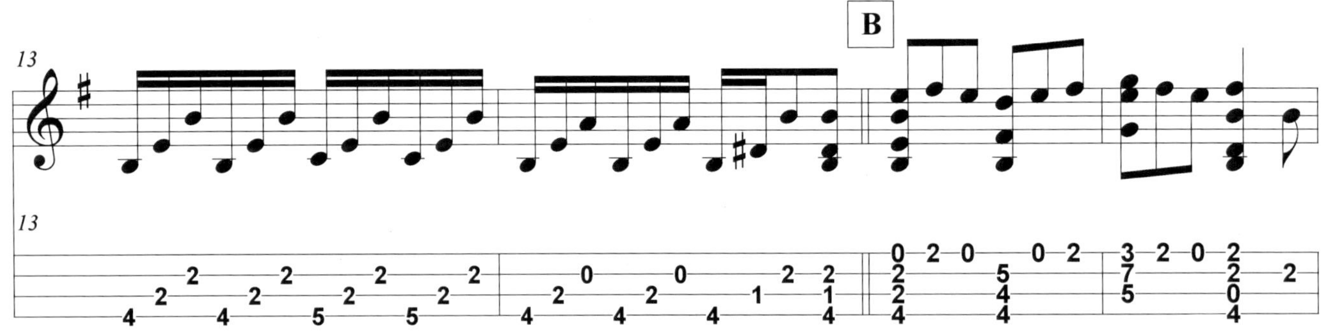

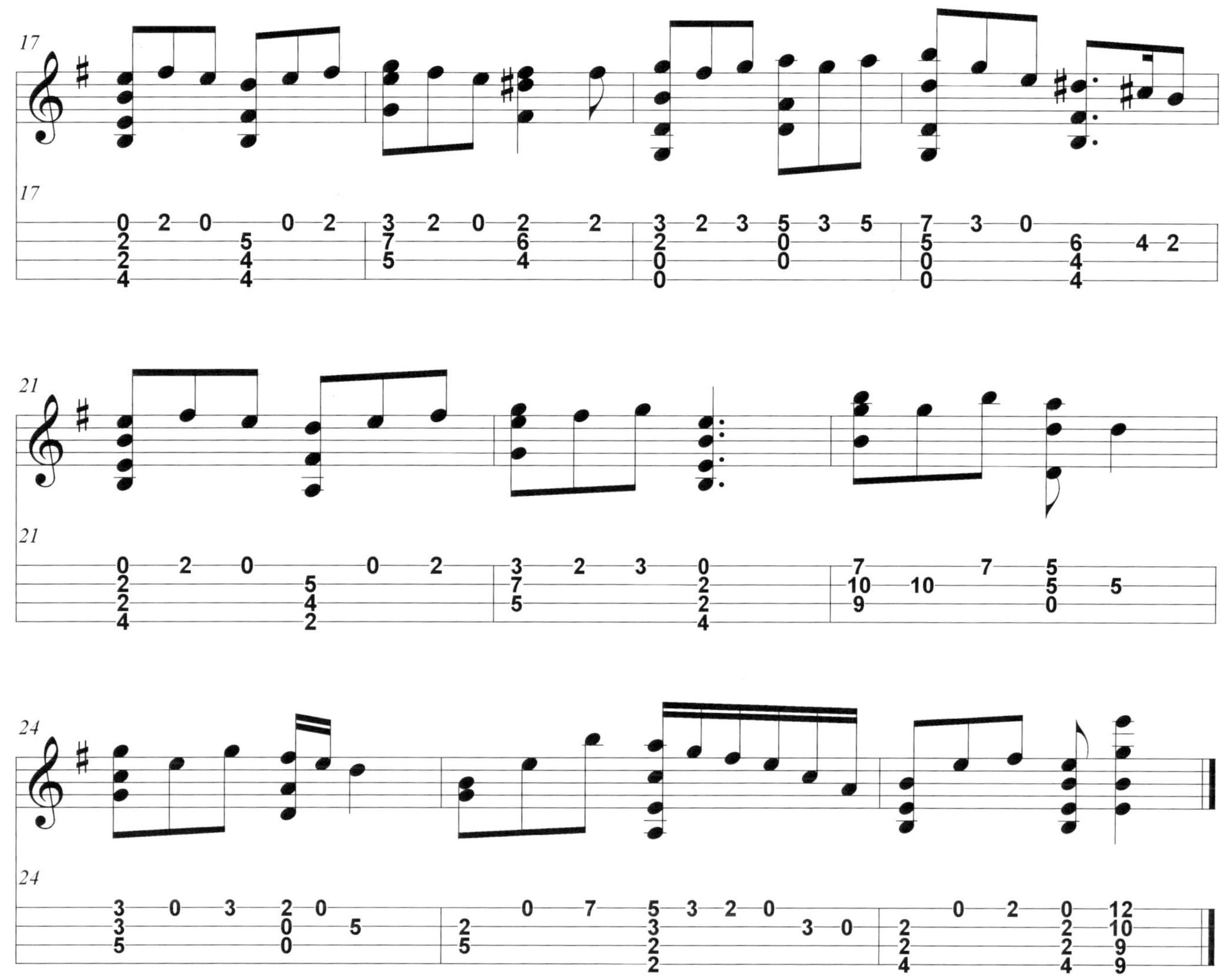

God Rest Ye Merry, Gentlemen

English Carol

Moderato 𝅗𝅥 = 85

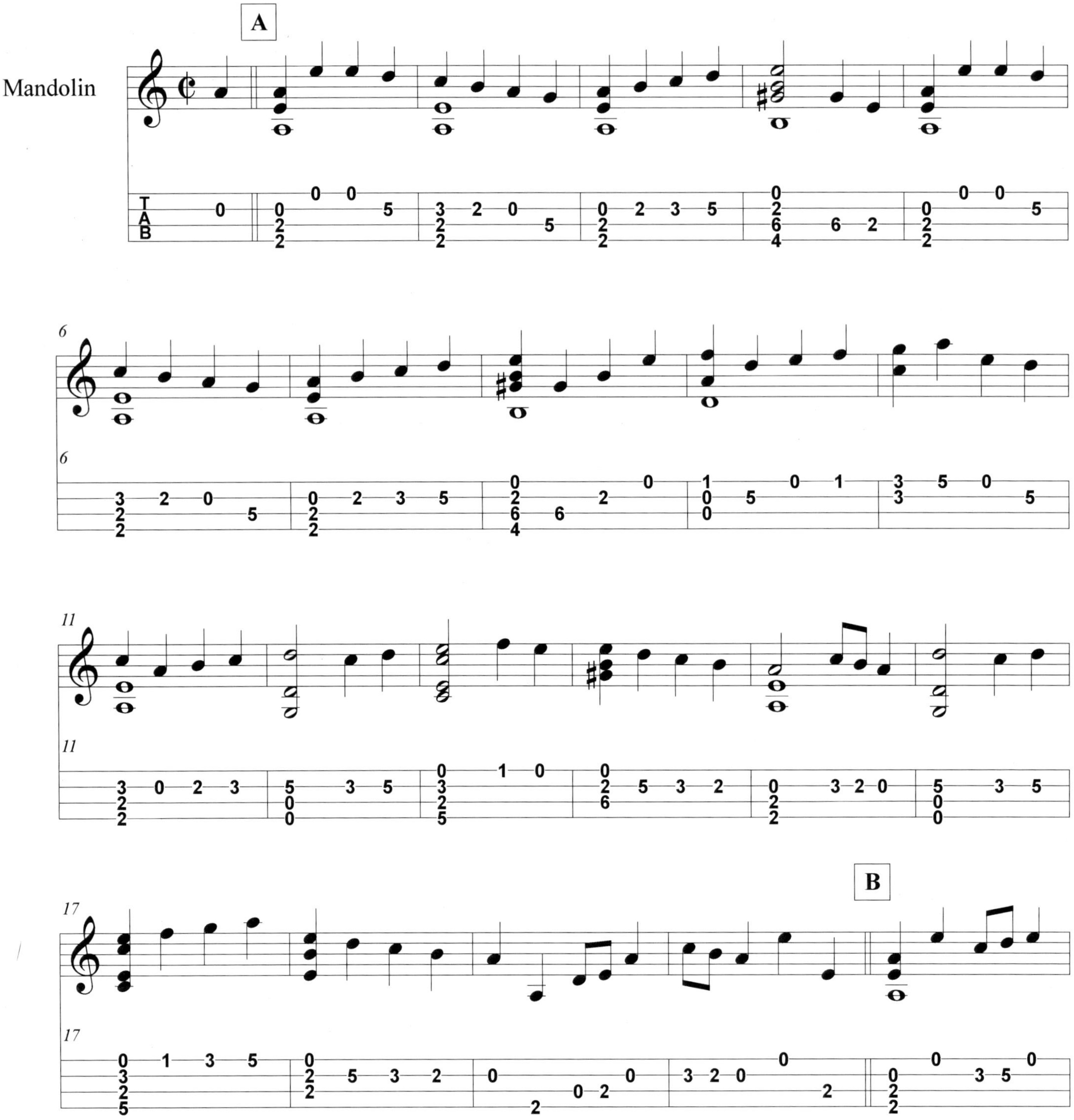

A

Mandolin

T
A
B

6

11

17

B

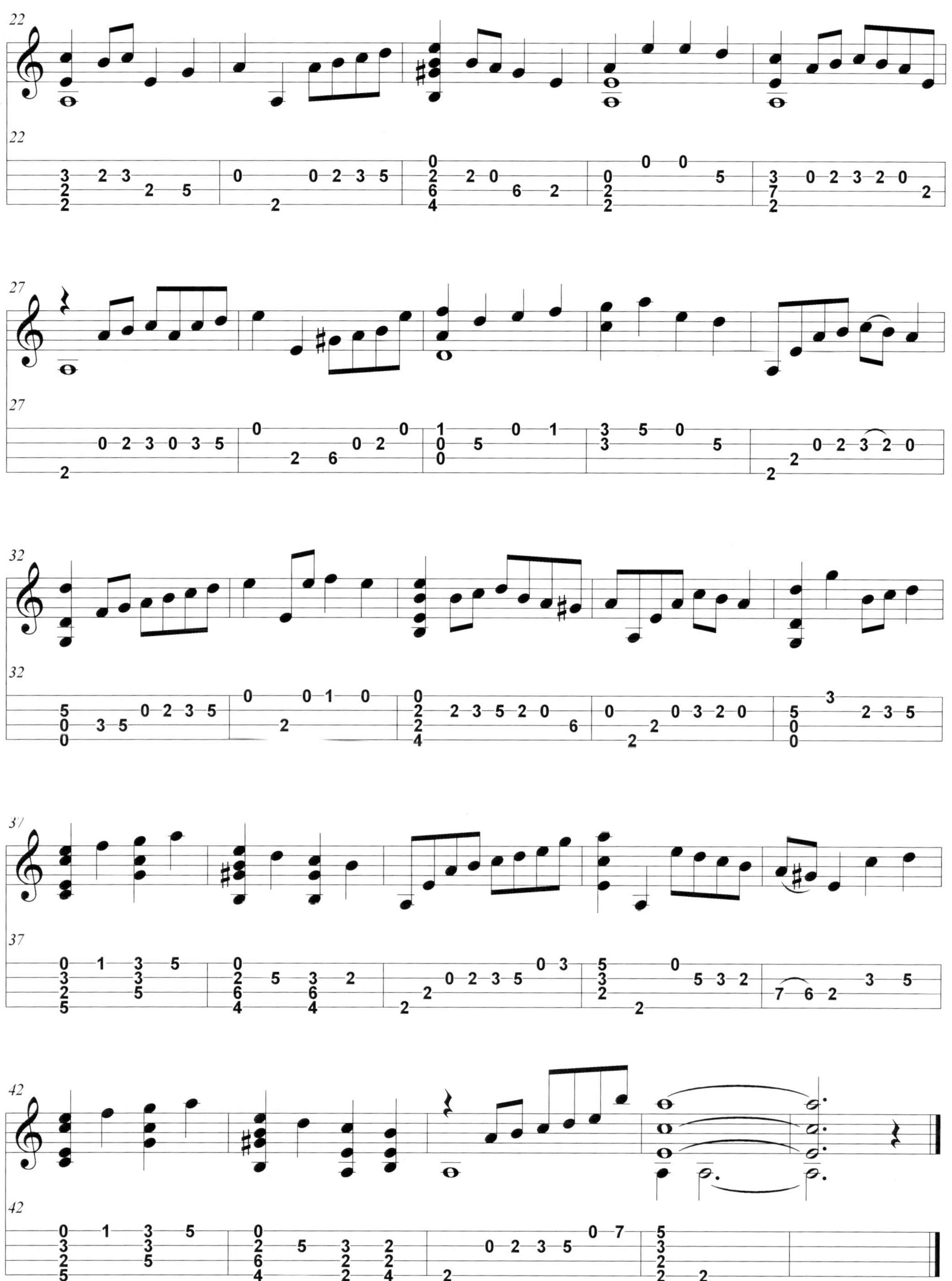

I Saw Three Ships

10

English Carol

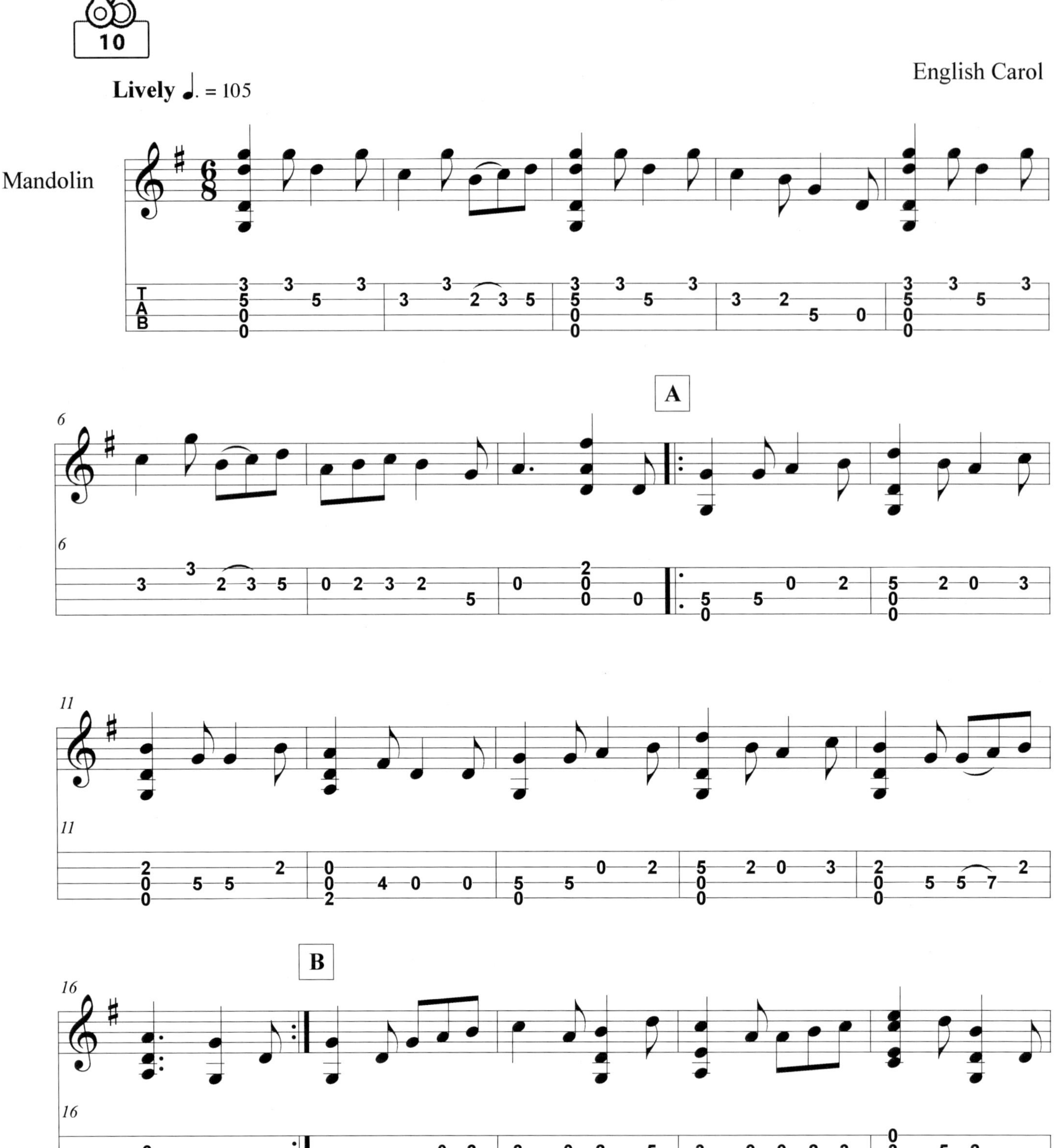

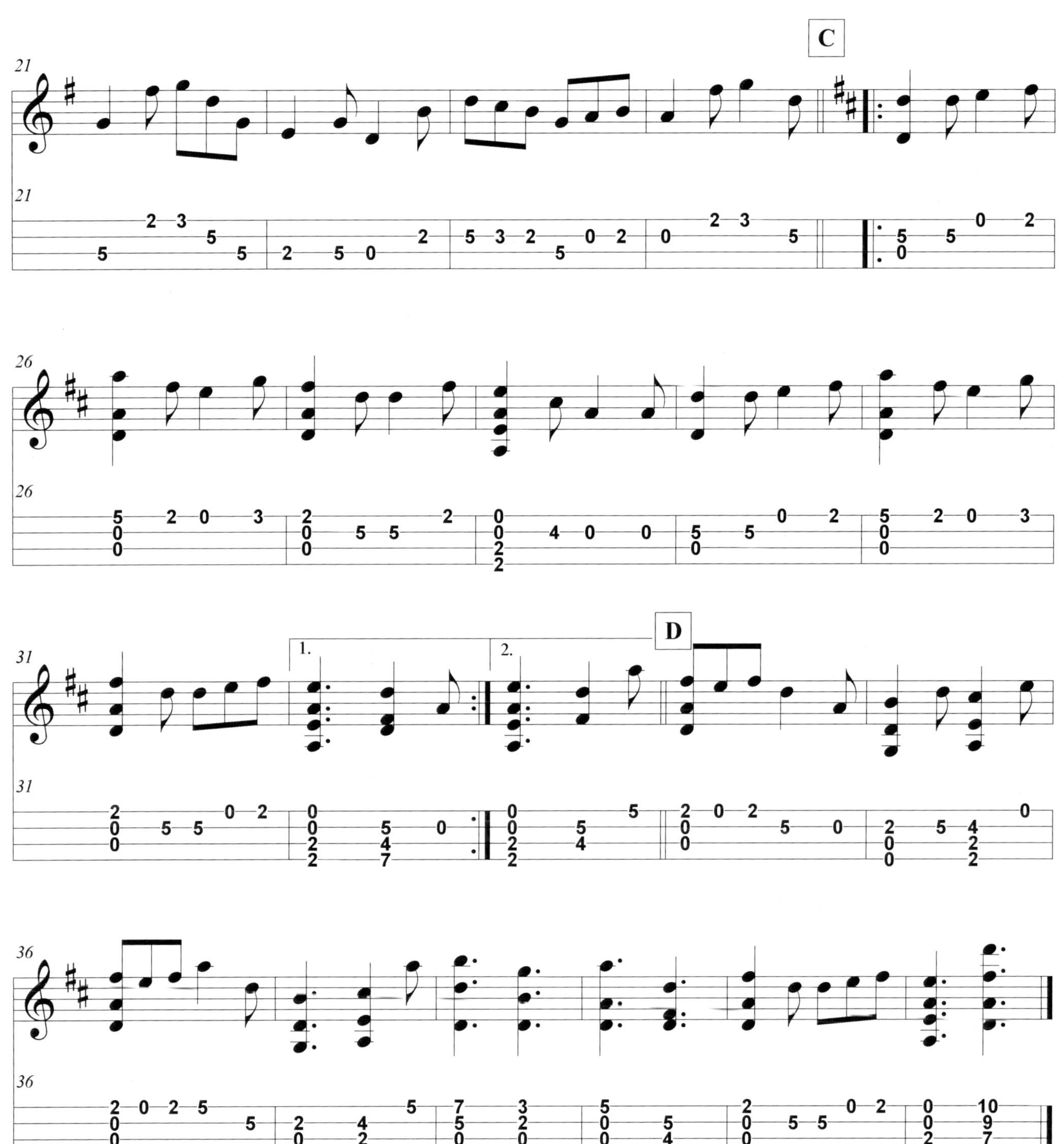
C
D
1.
2.

What Child is This?

With Expression ♩ = 120

English Carol

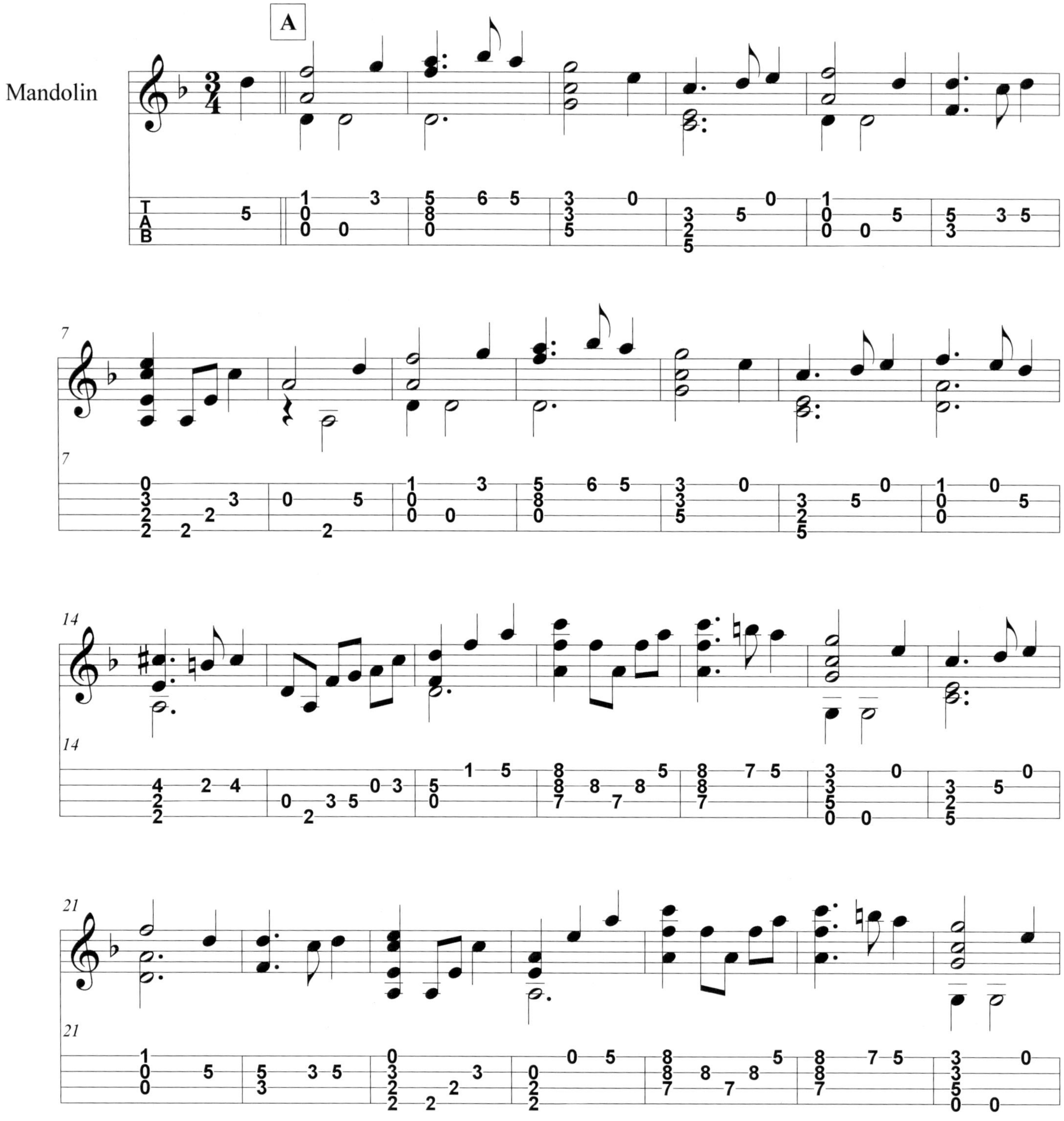

Mandolin

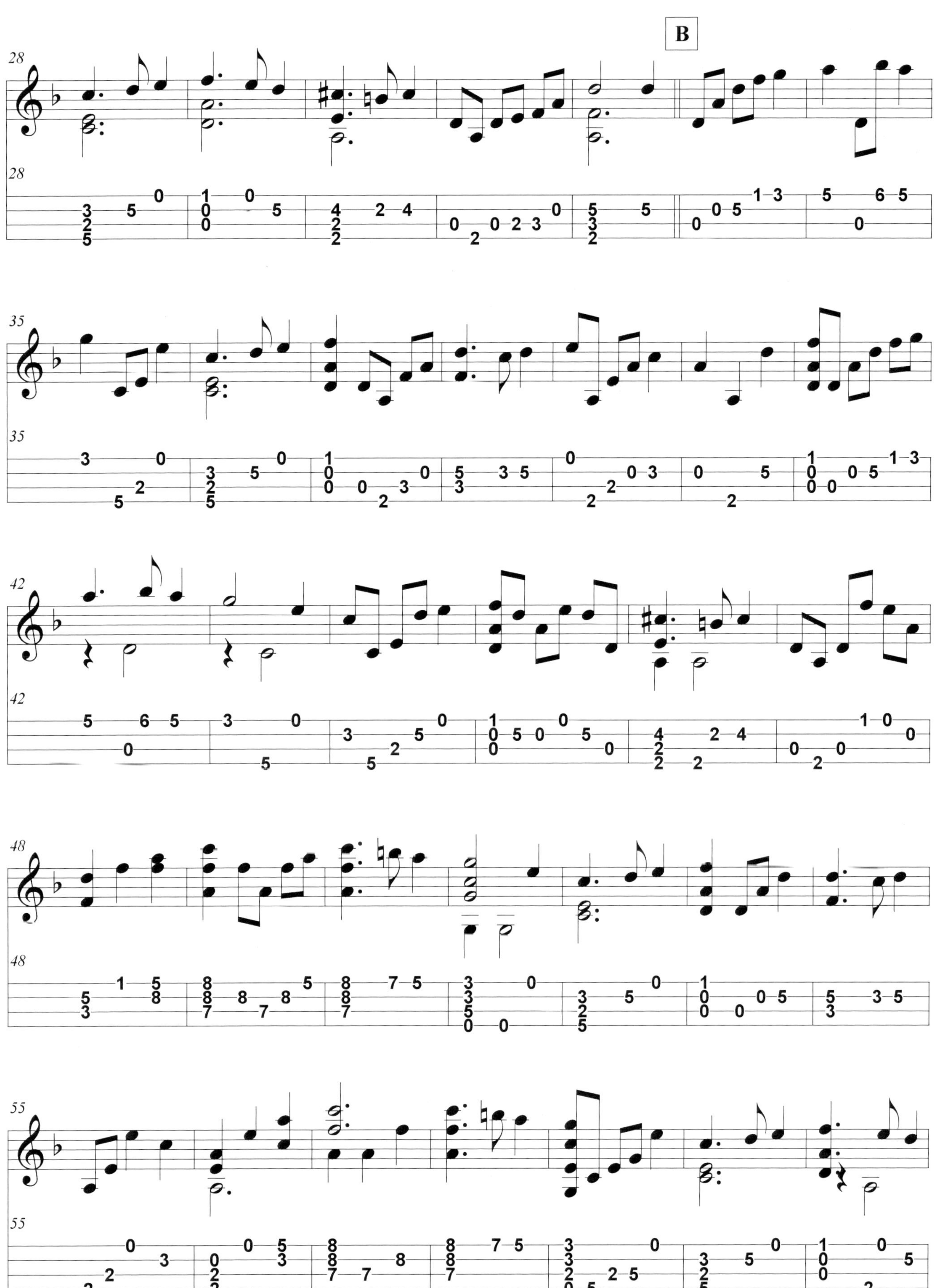
B

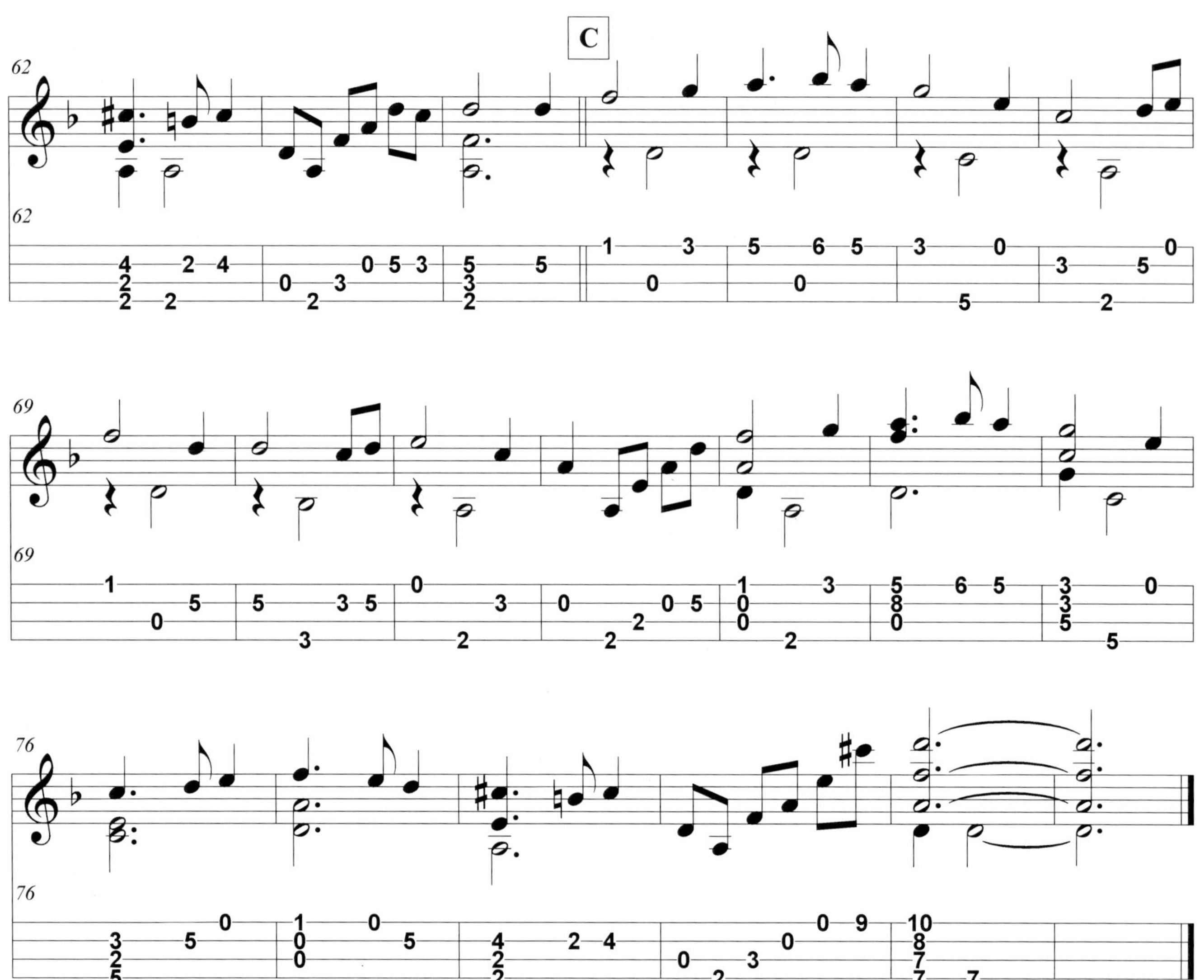
C

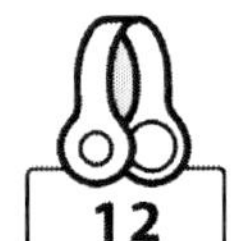

In the Bleak Midwinter

Gustav Holst

Adagio ♩ = 66

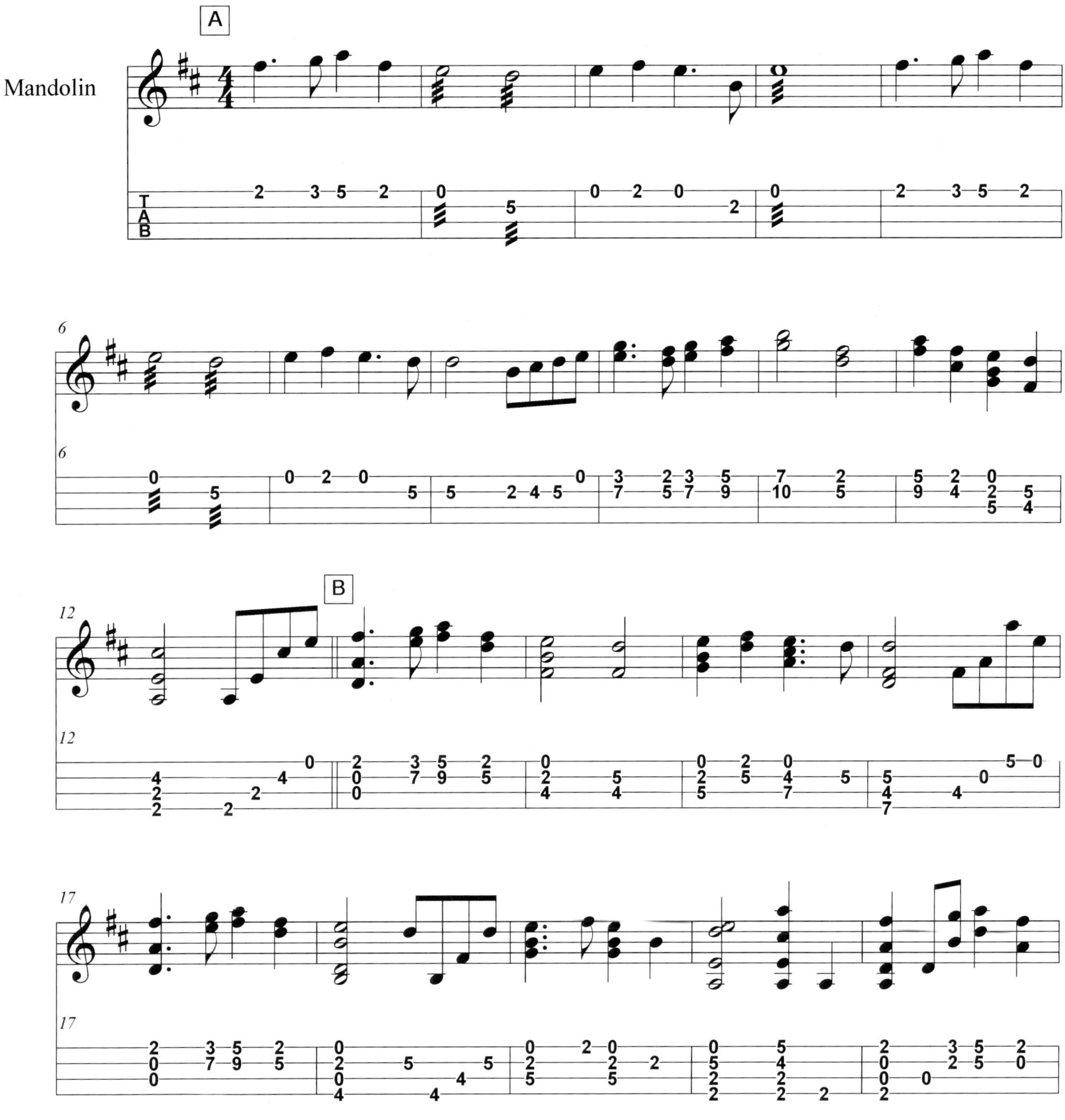

A

Mandolin

6

6

12

B

12

17

17

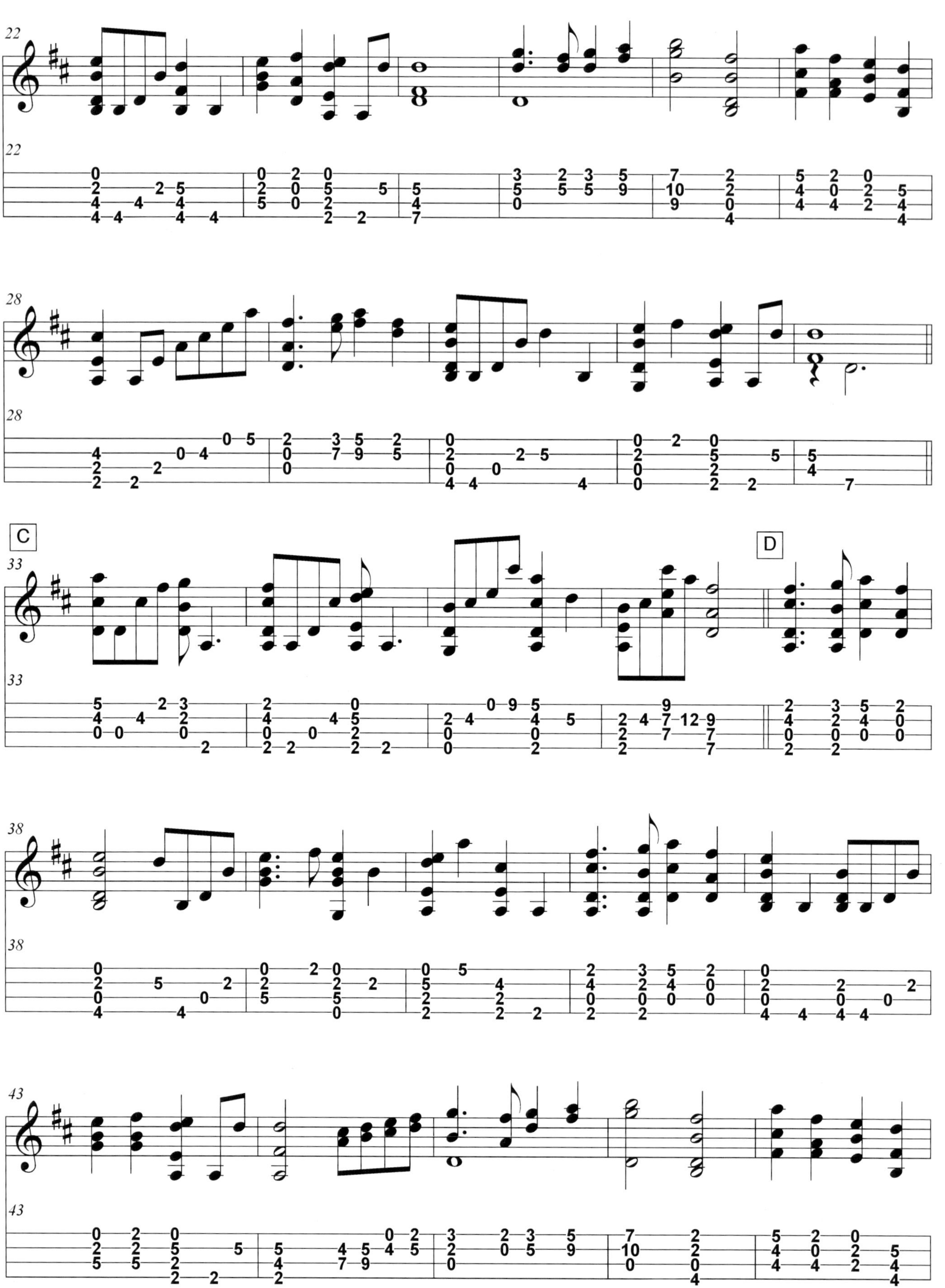

C
D

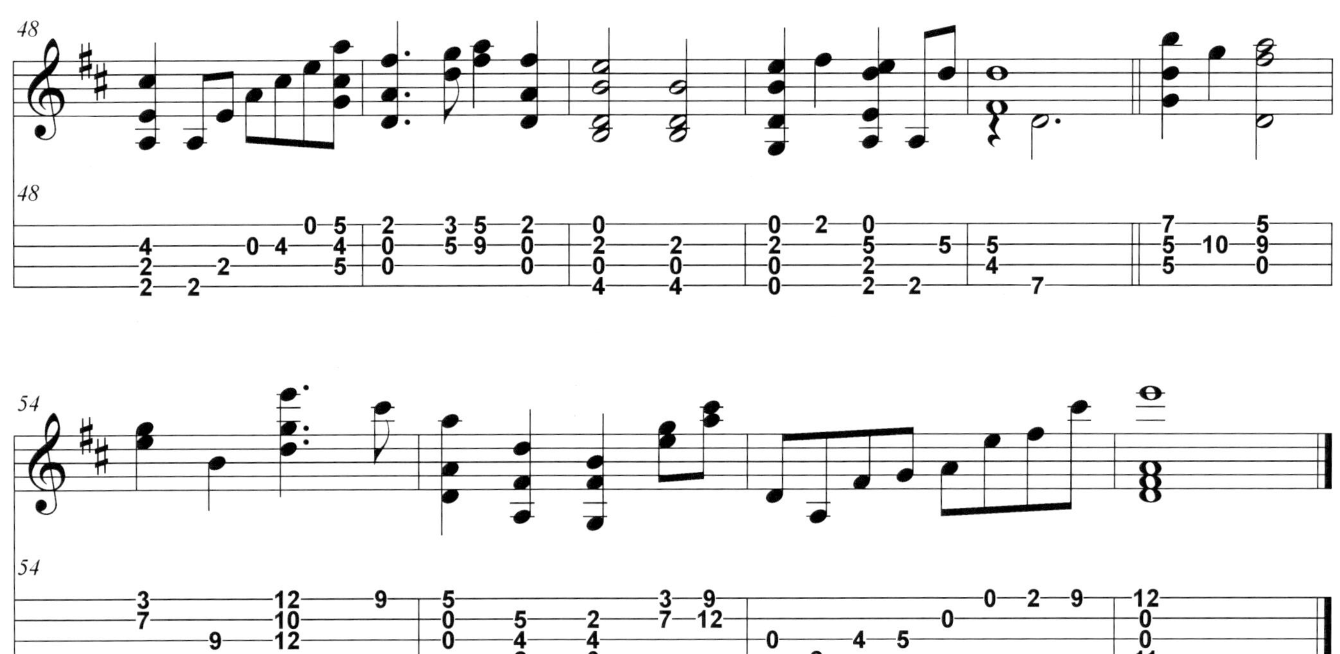

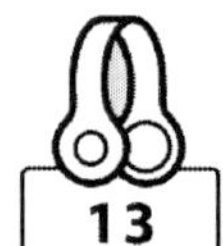

My Dancing Day

Moderato 𝅗𝅥. = 50

English Carol

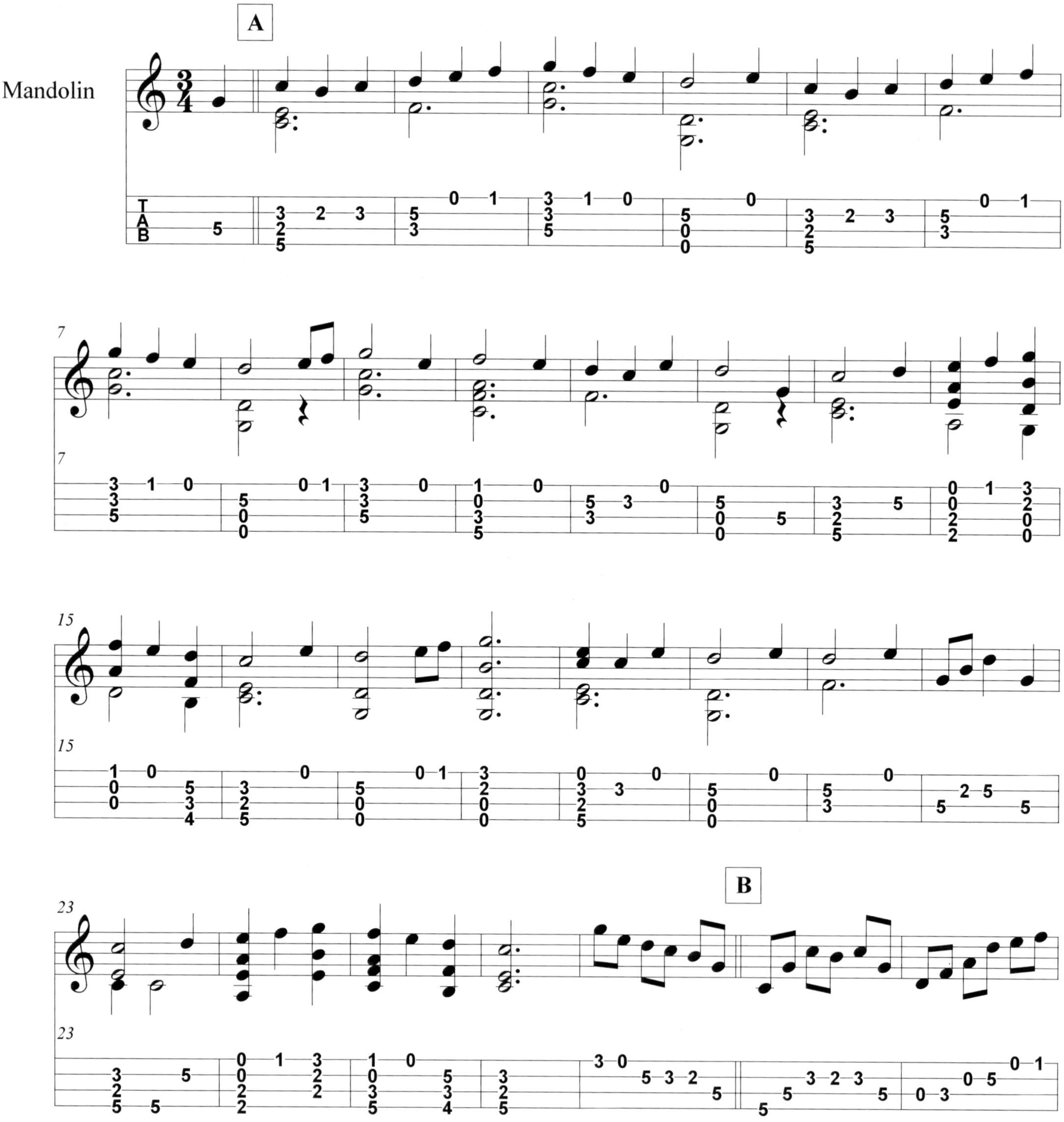

A

Mandolin

B

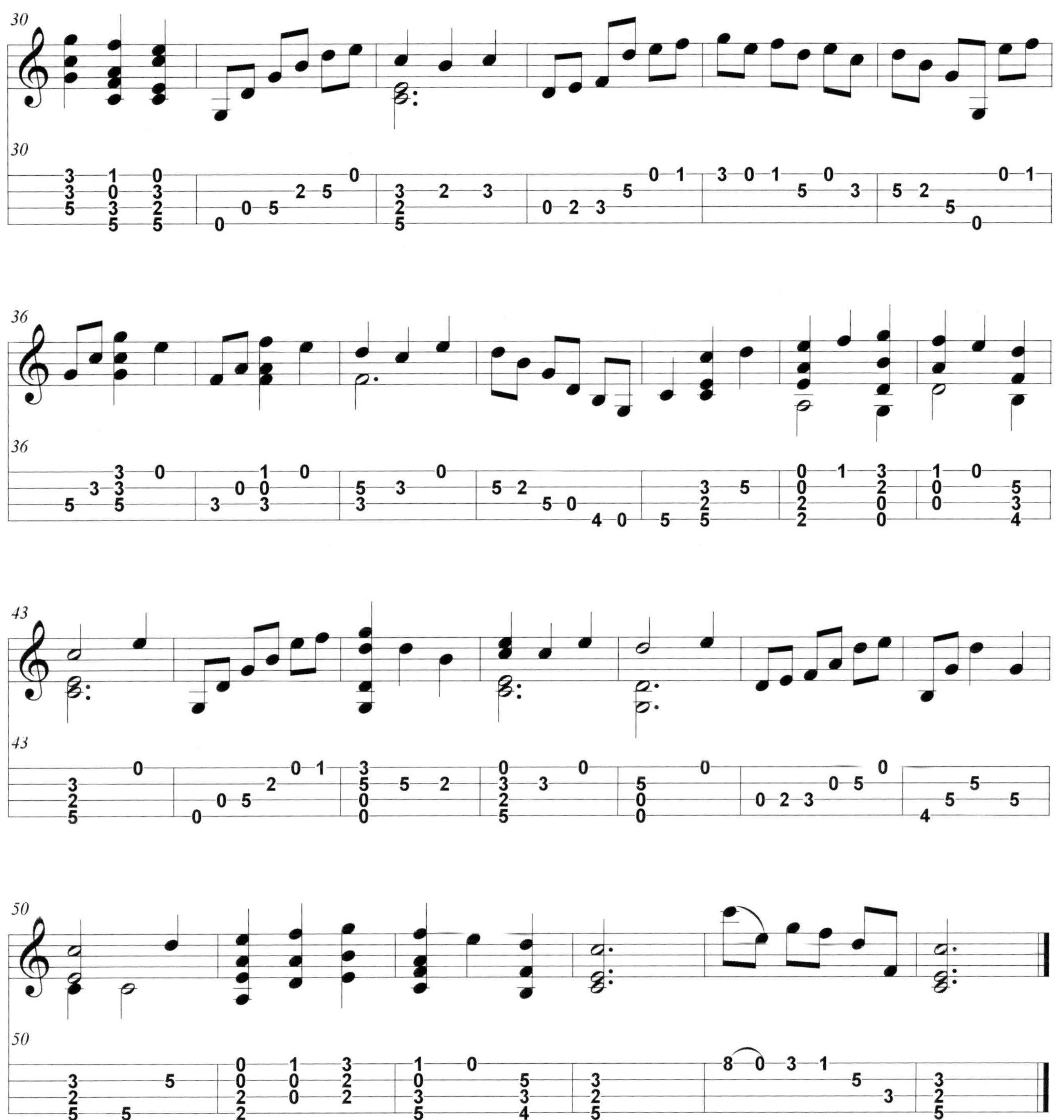

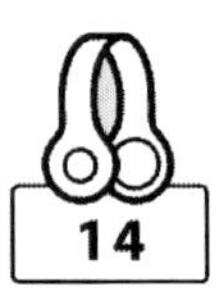

On Christmas Night

Sussex Carol

Joyfully ♩. = 80

English Carol

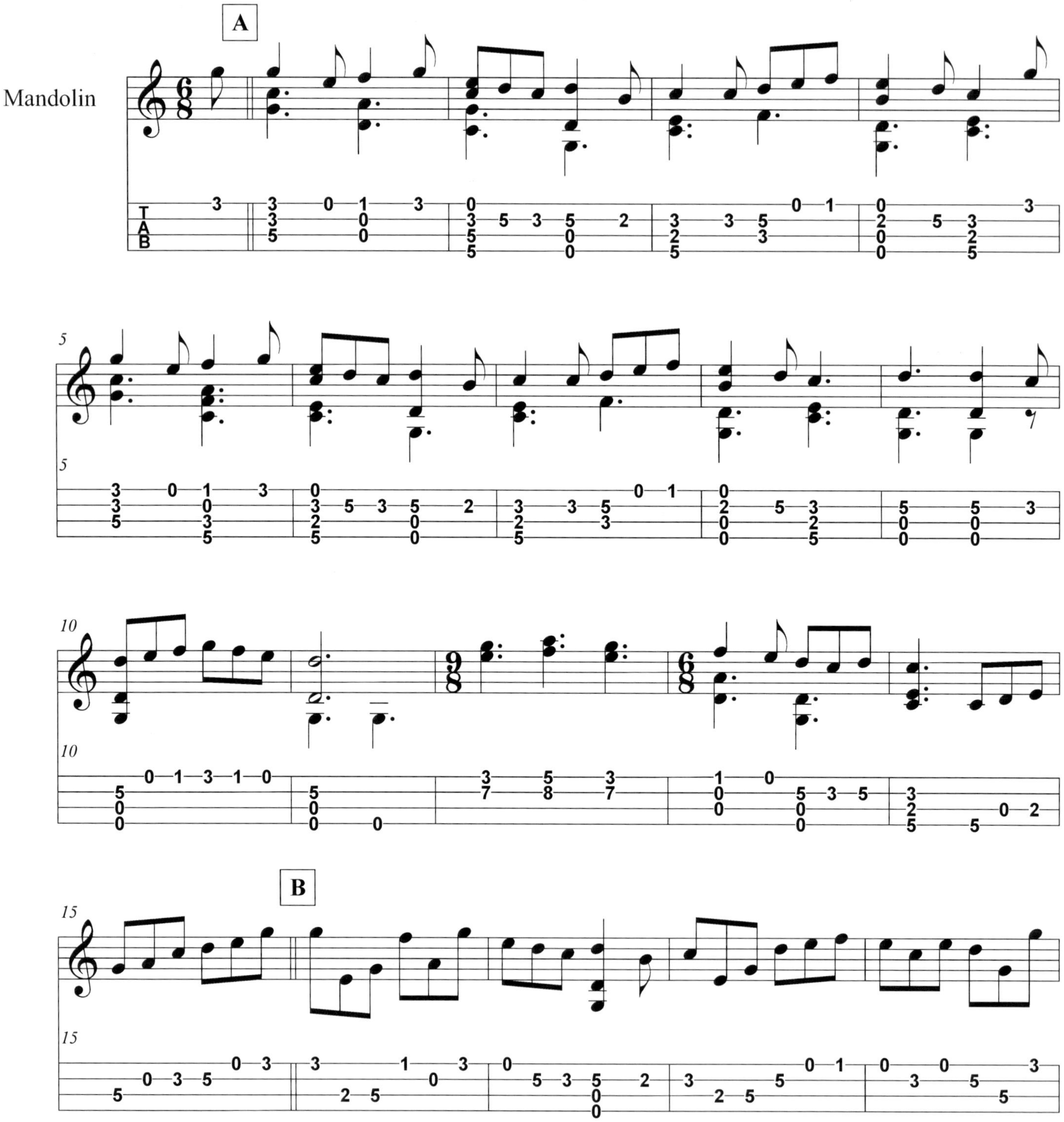

Mandolin

A

B

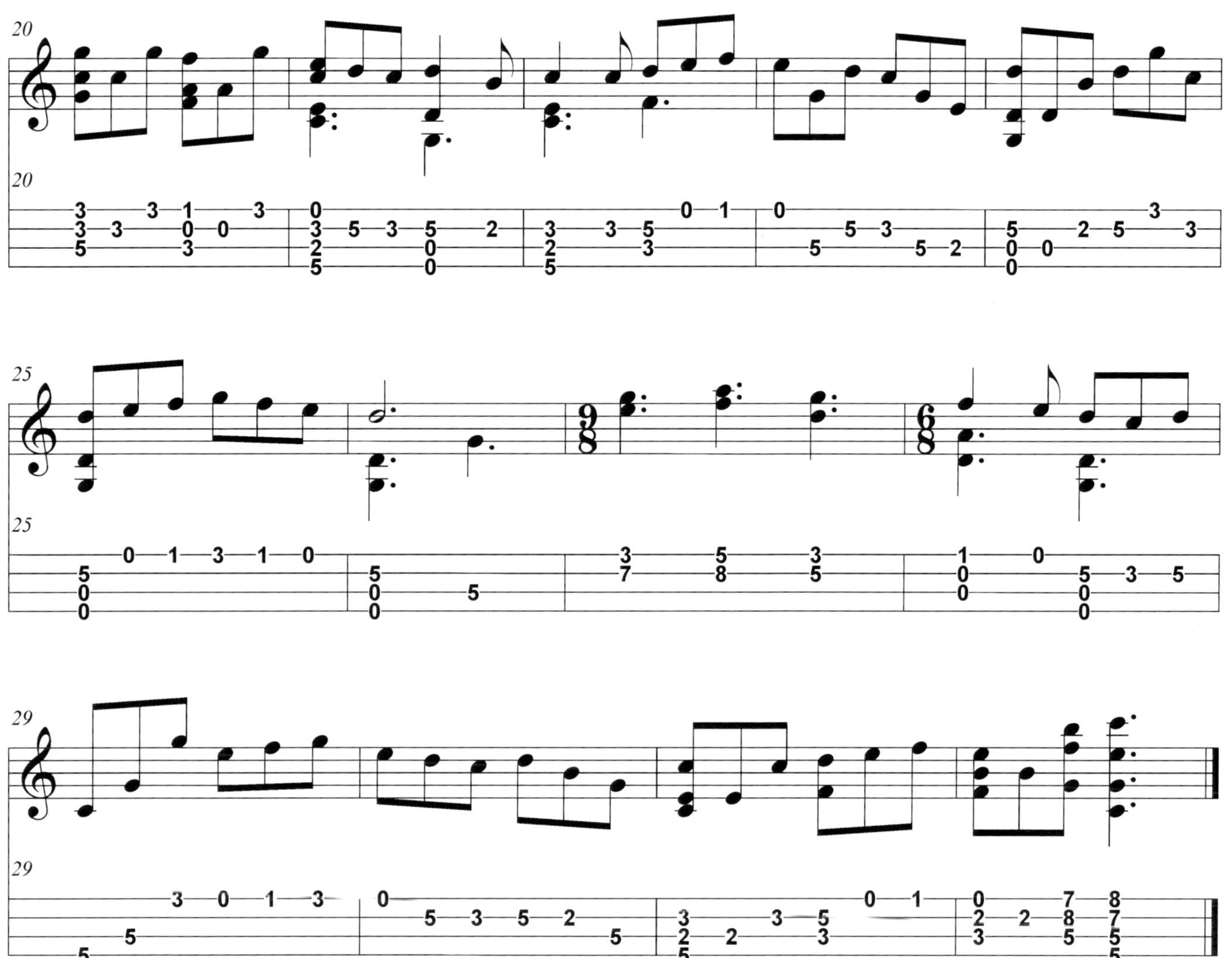

Once in Royal David's City

Henry John Gauntlett

Moderato ♩ = 88

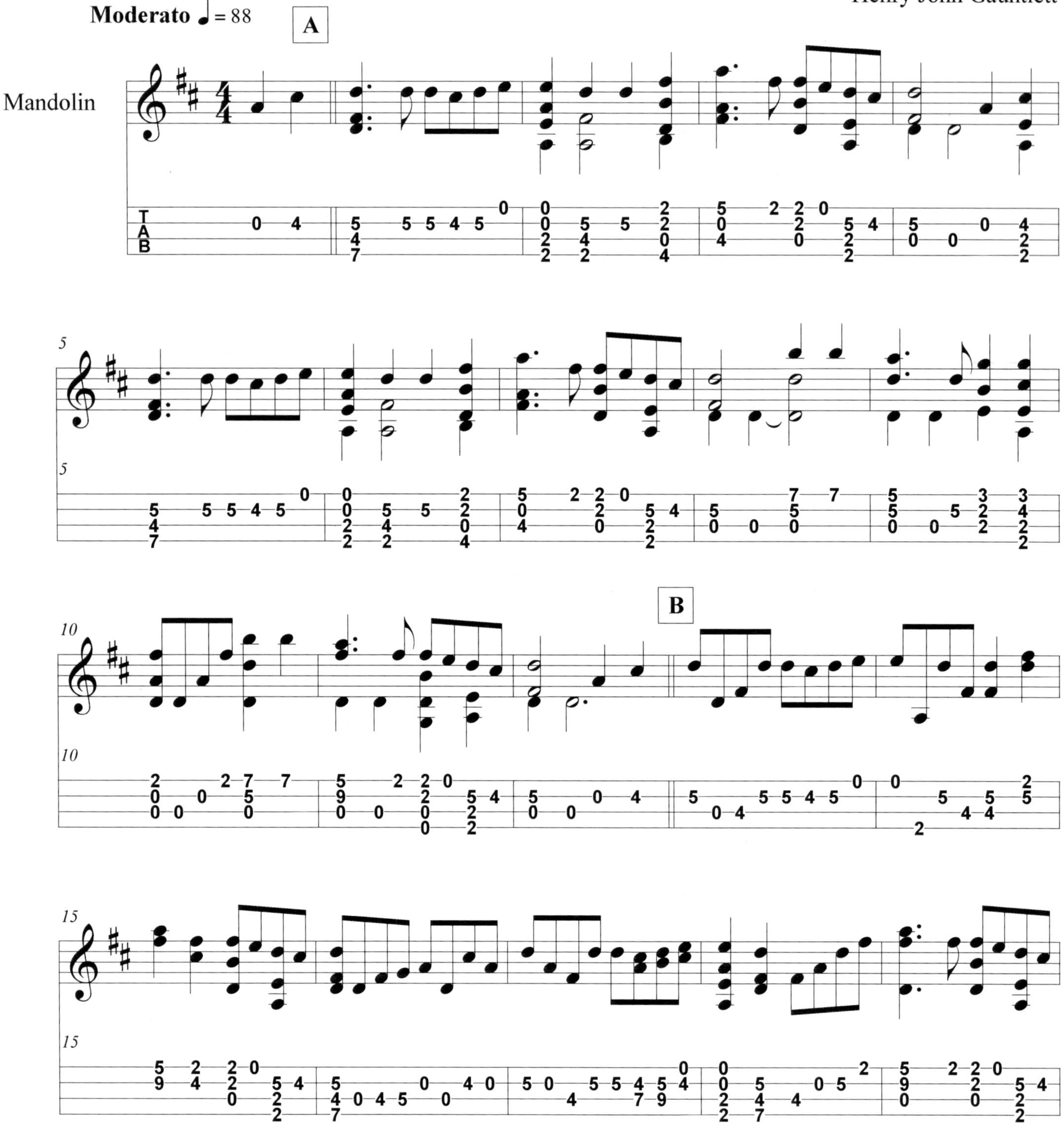

A

Mandolin

B

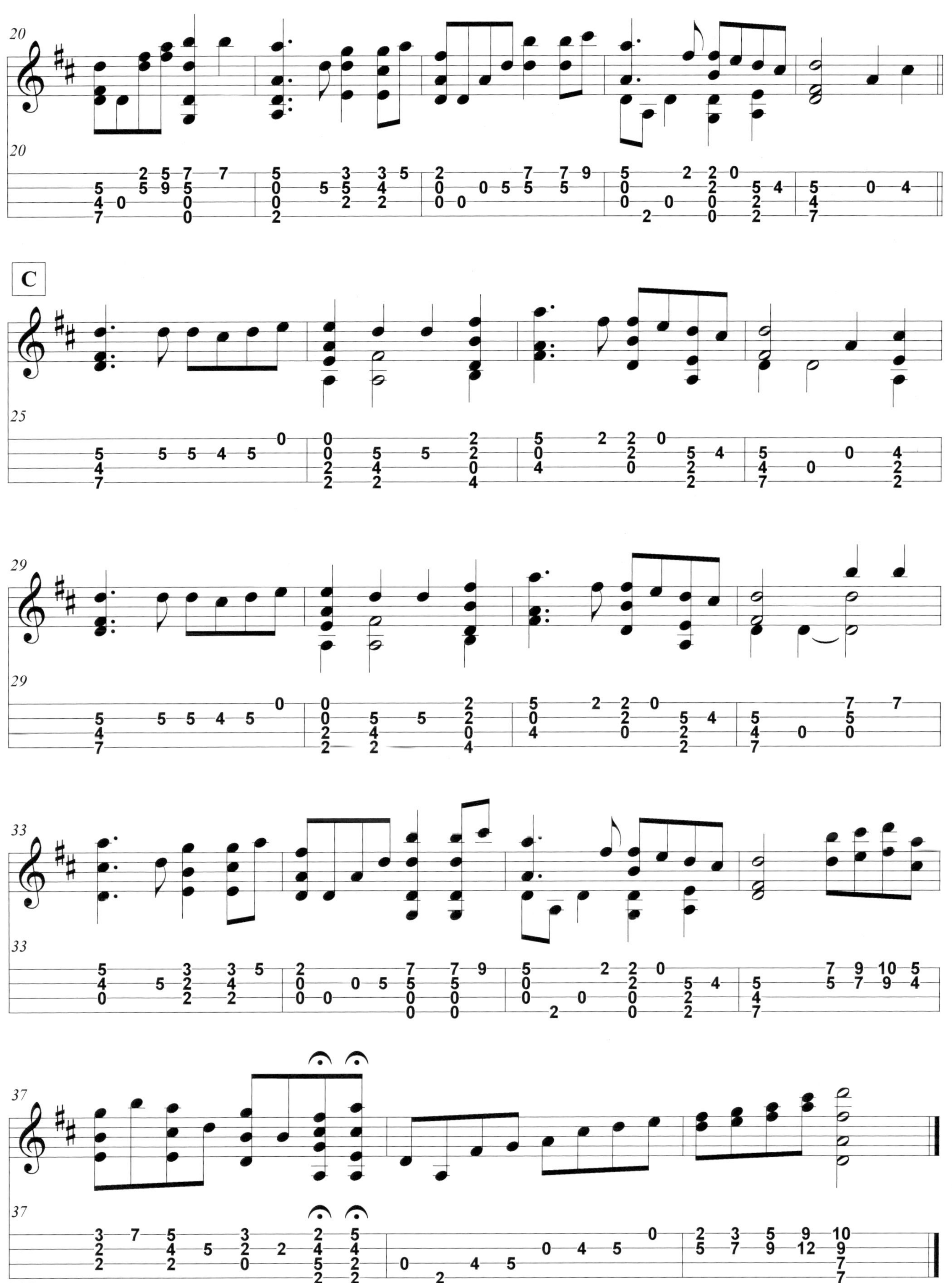
C

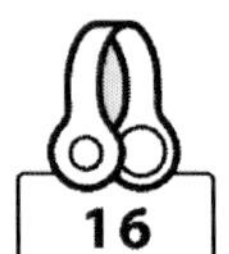

Remember

16th Century English

Freely 𝅗𝅥. = 82

A

Mandolin

5

9

13

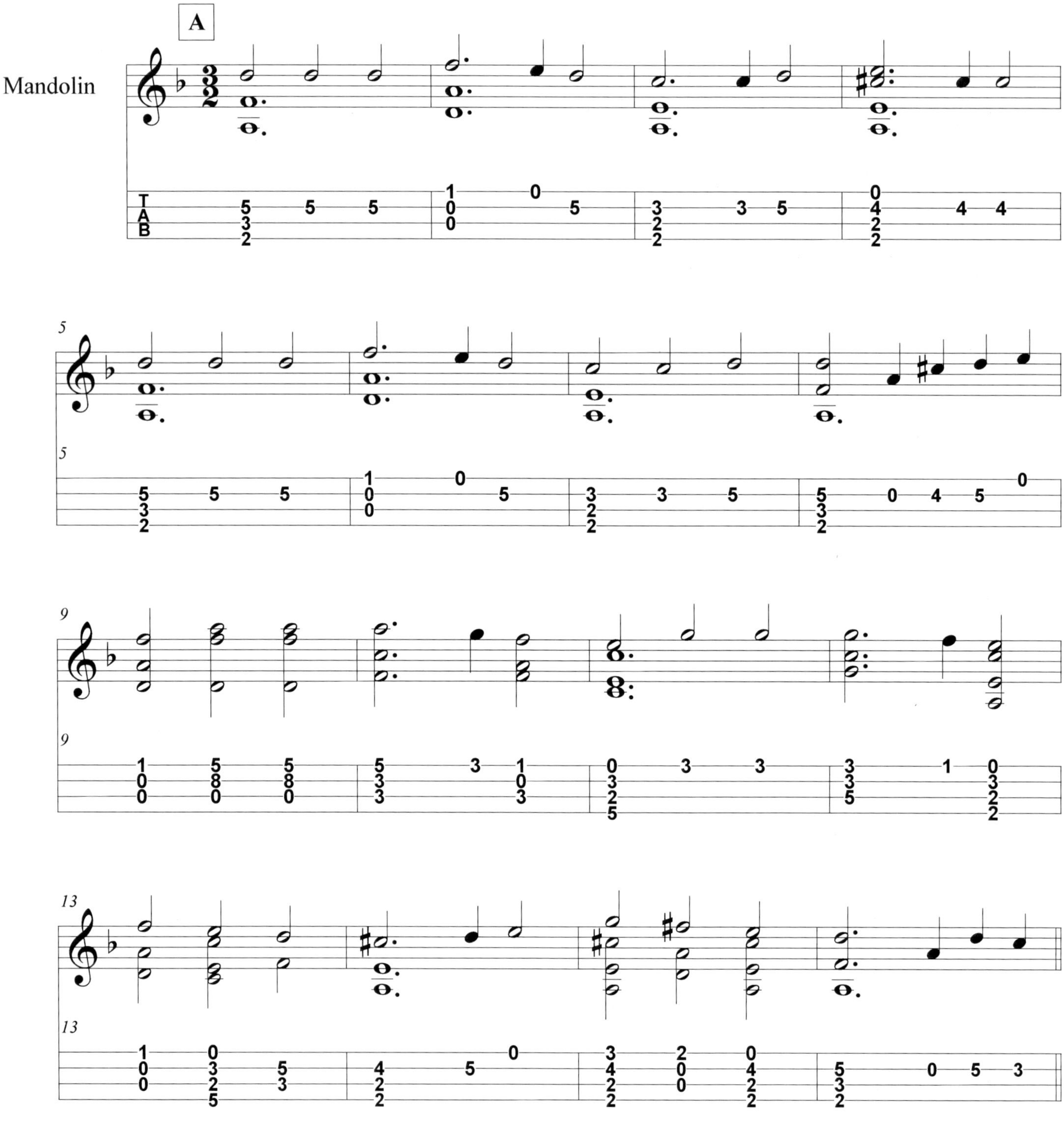

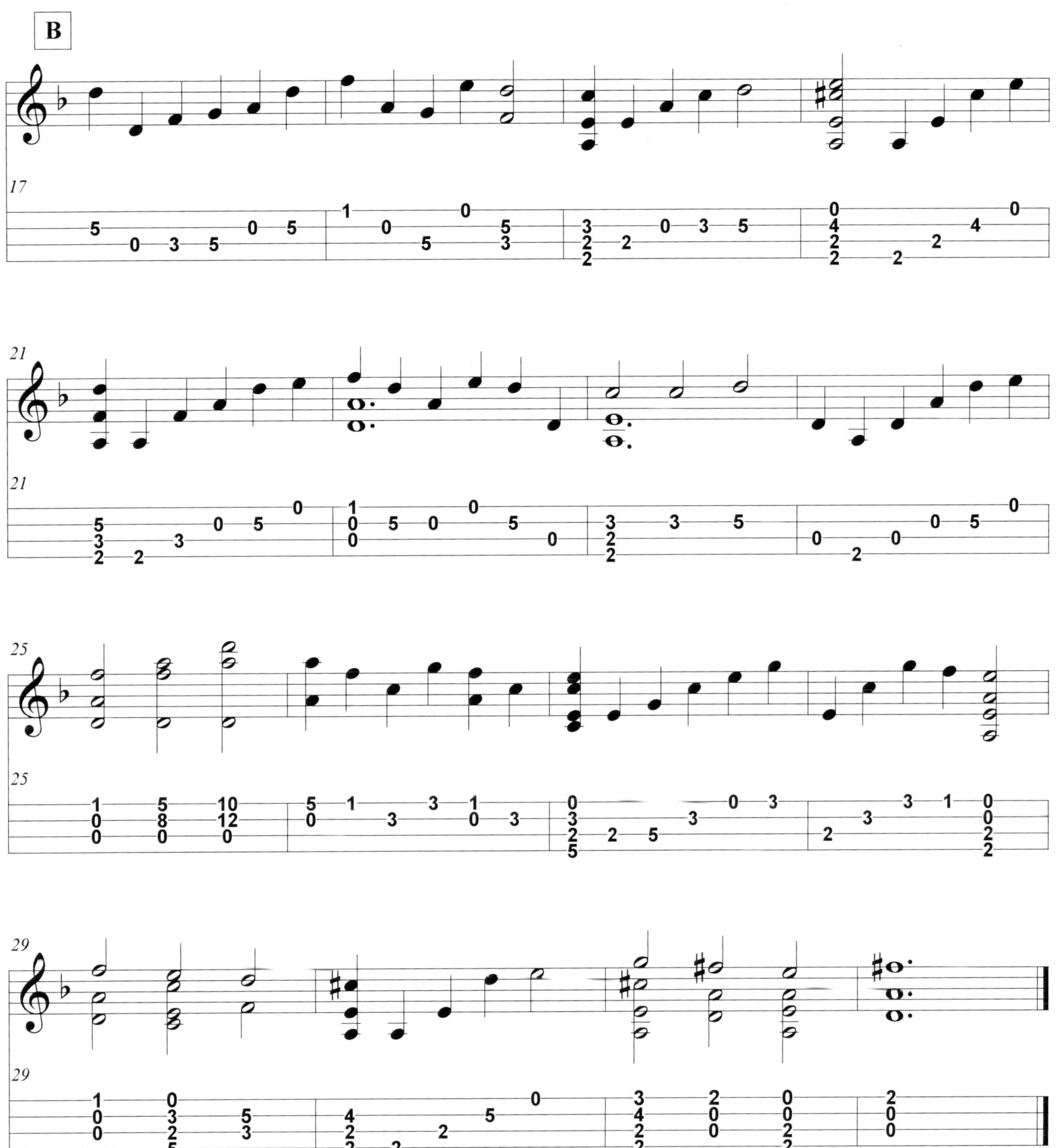
B
17
21
25
29

The Bagpiper's Carol

17

Joyfully ♩. = 80

Scottish Carol

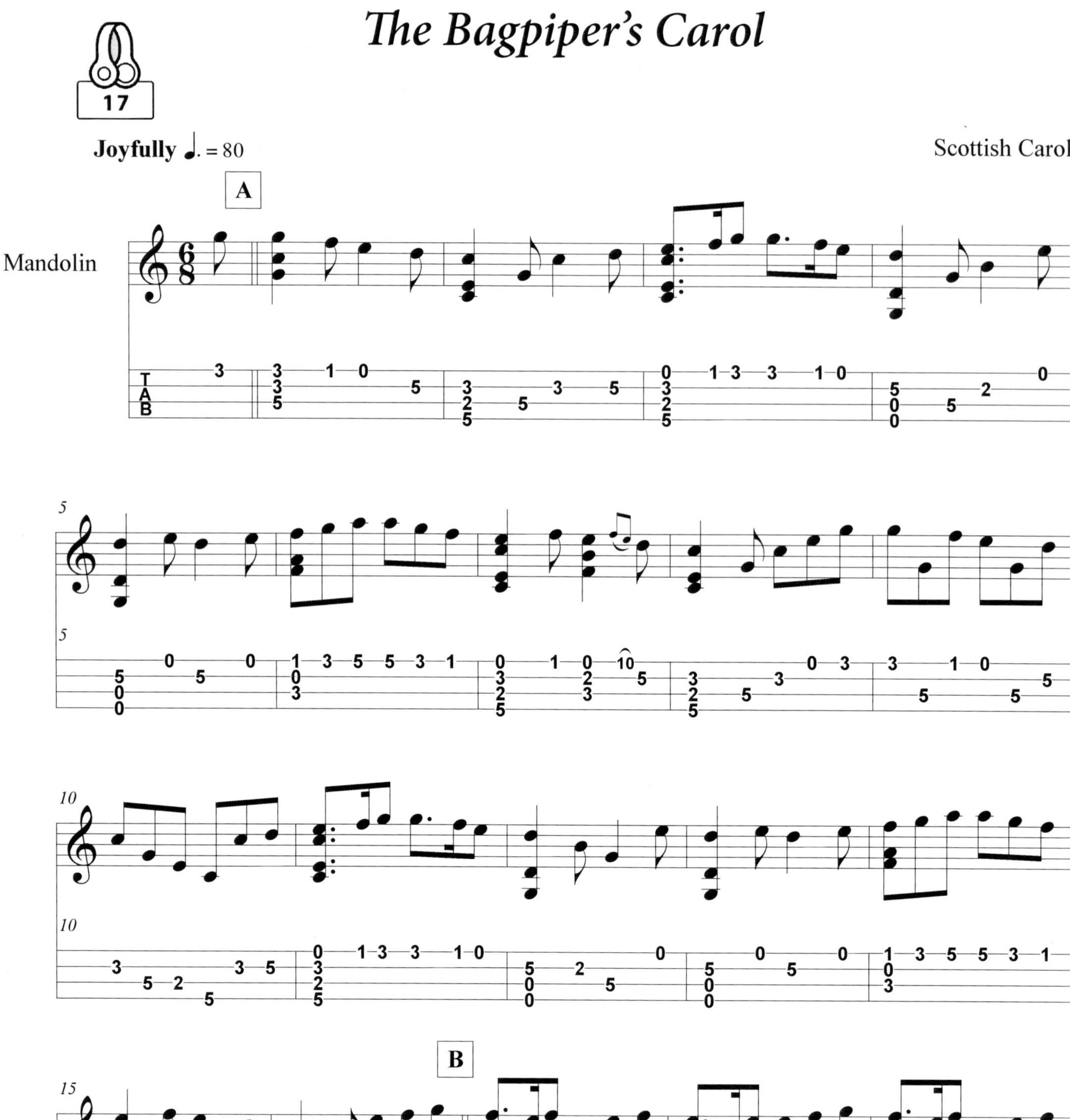

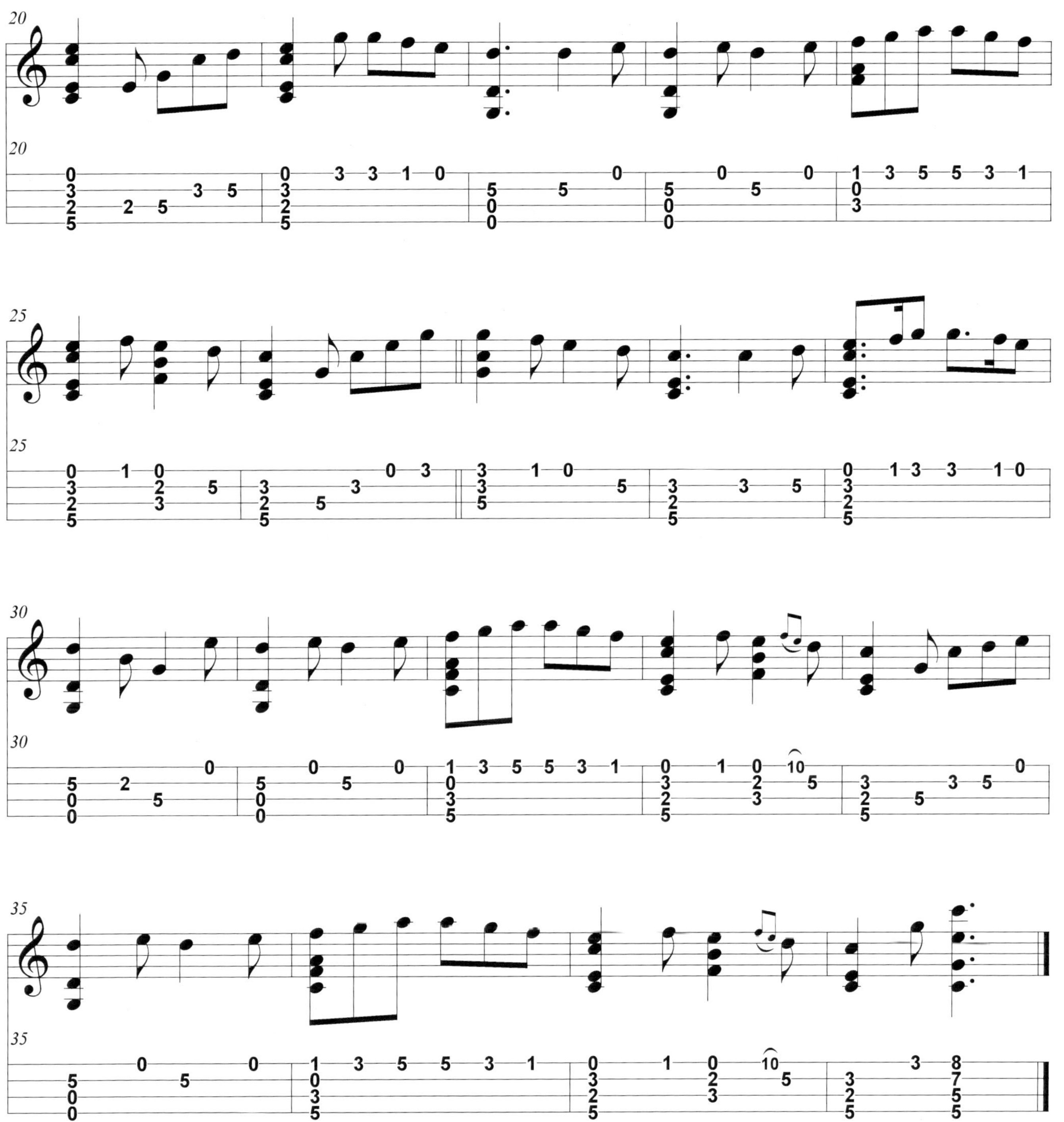

The Devonshire Carol/The Moon Shines Bright

Medley

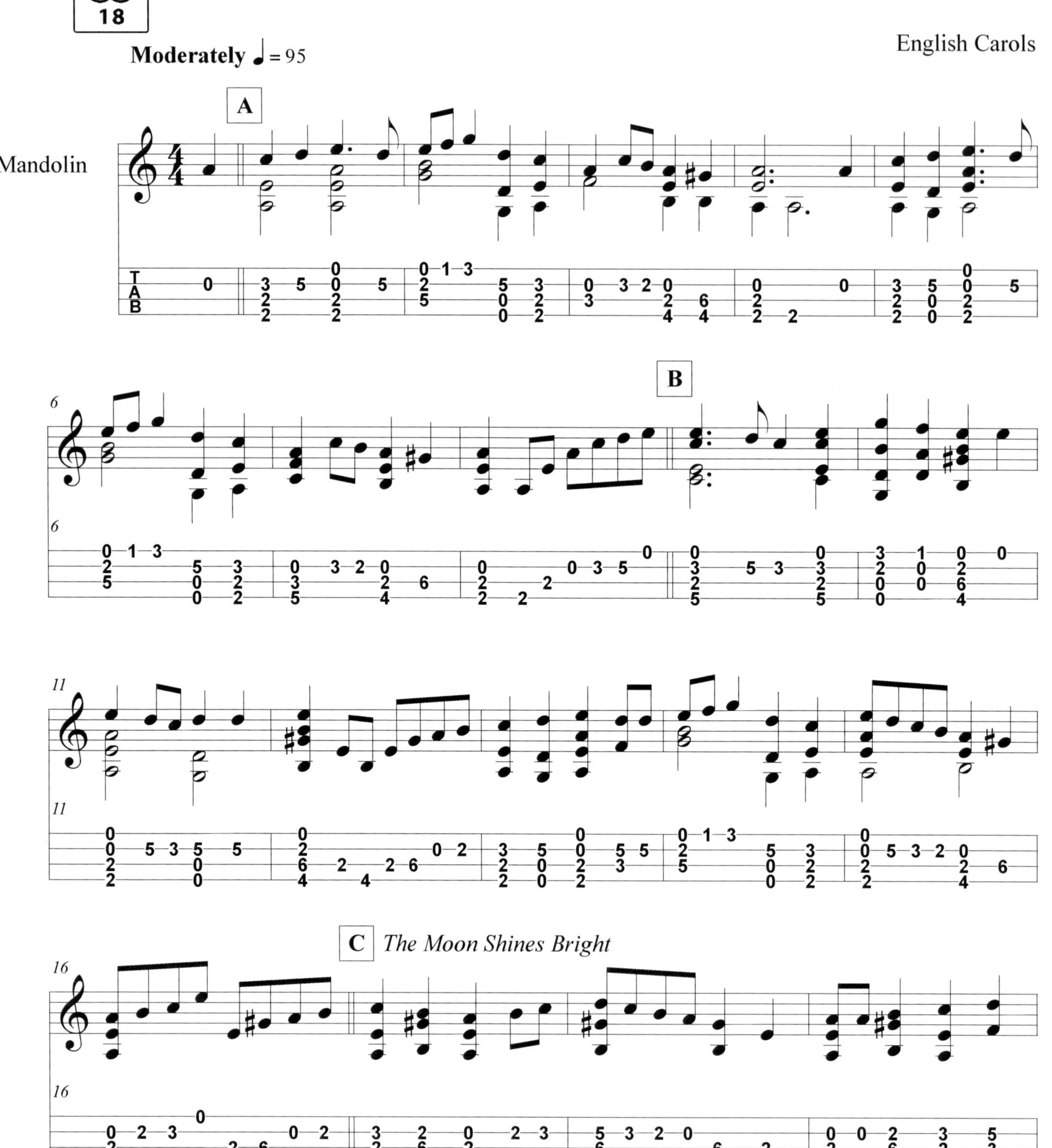

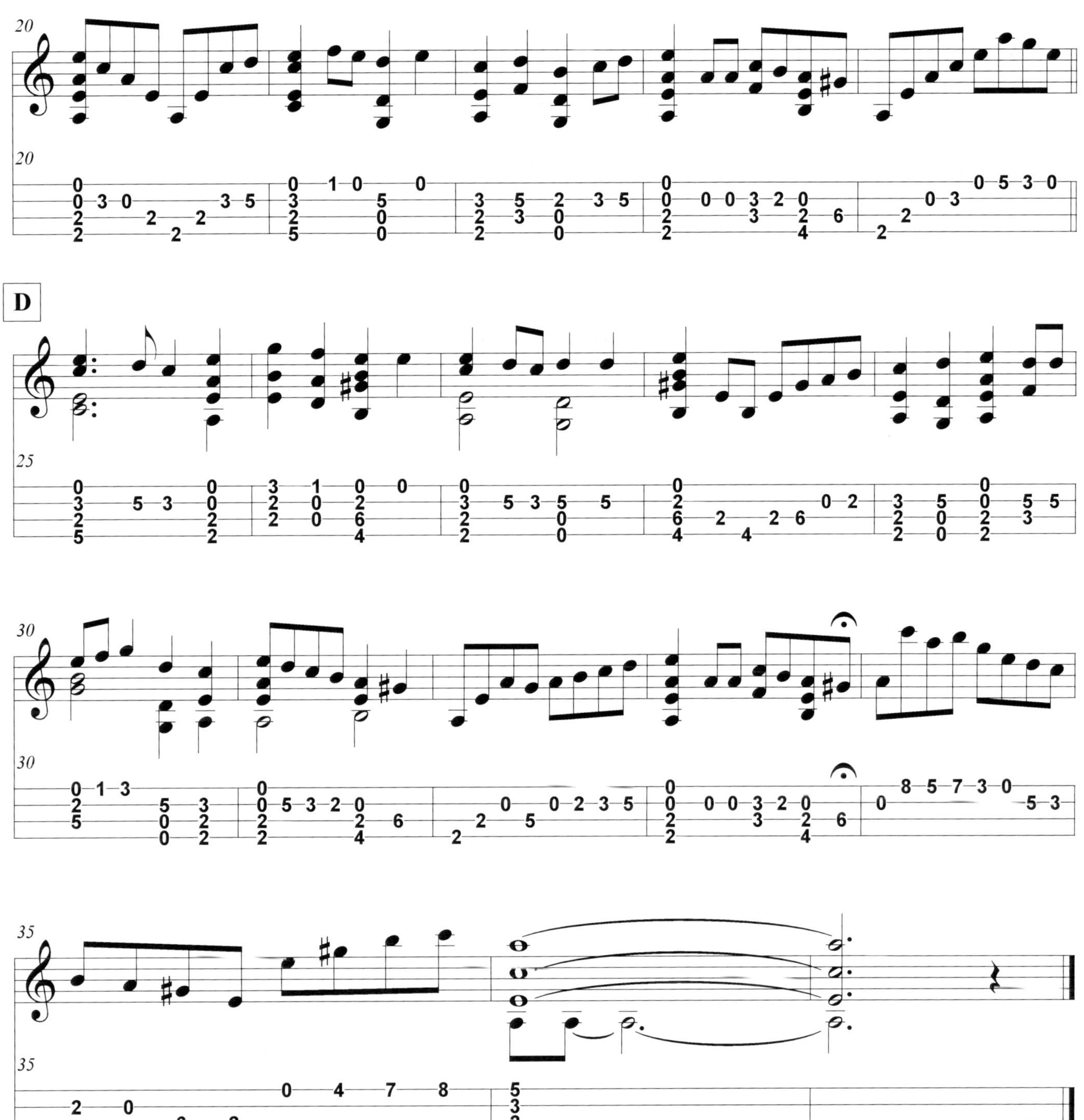
D

Wexford Carol

Irish Carol

Freely ♩ = 74

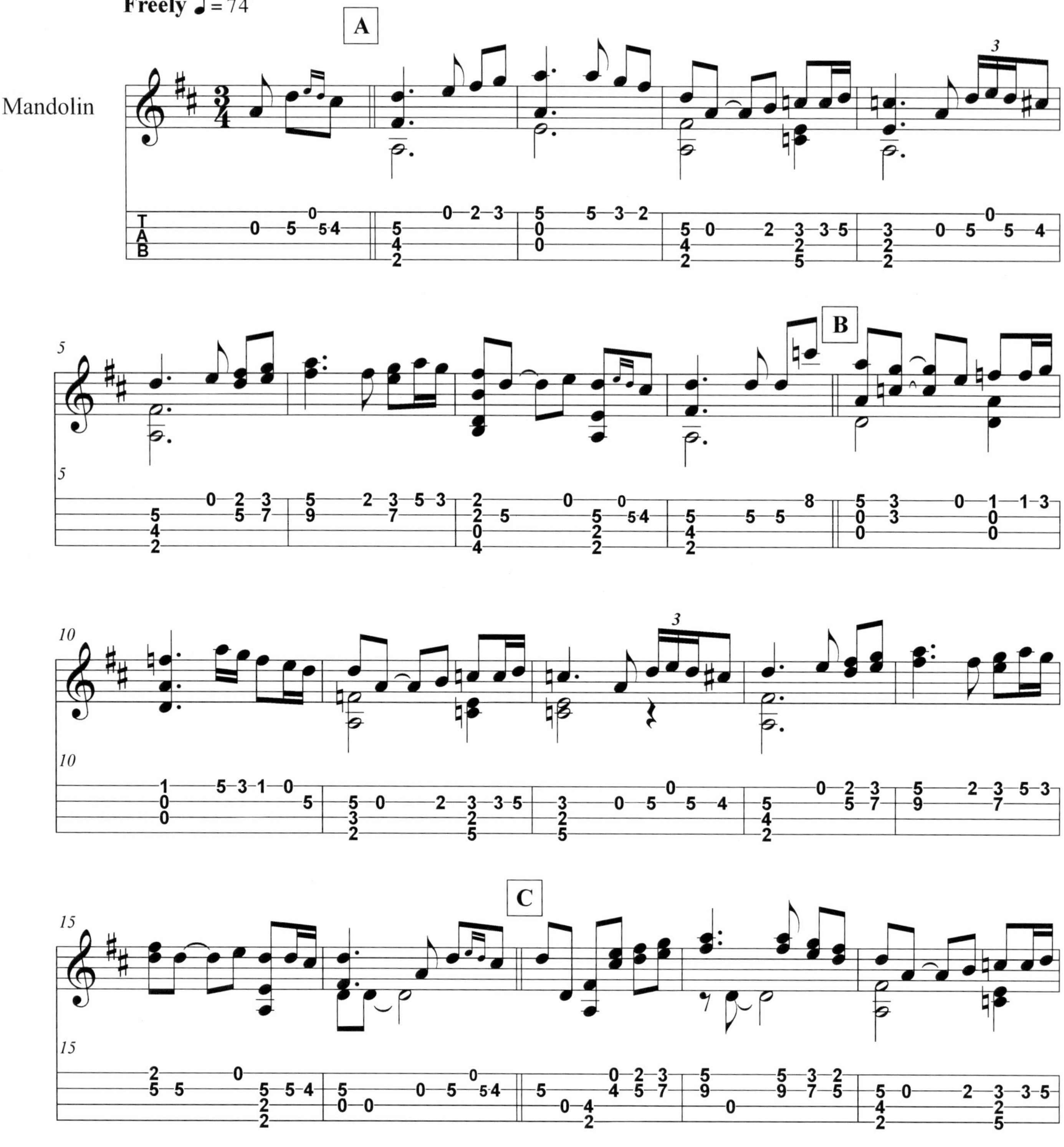

A

Mandolin

5

B

10

15

C

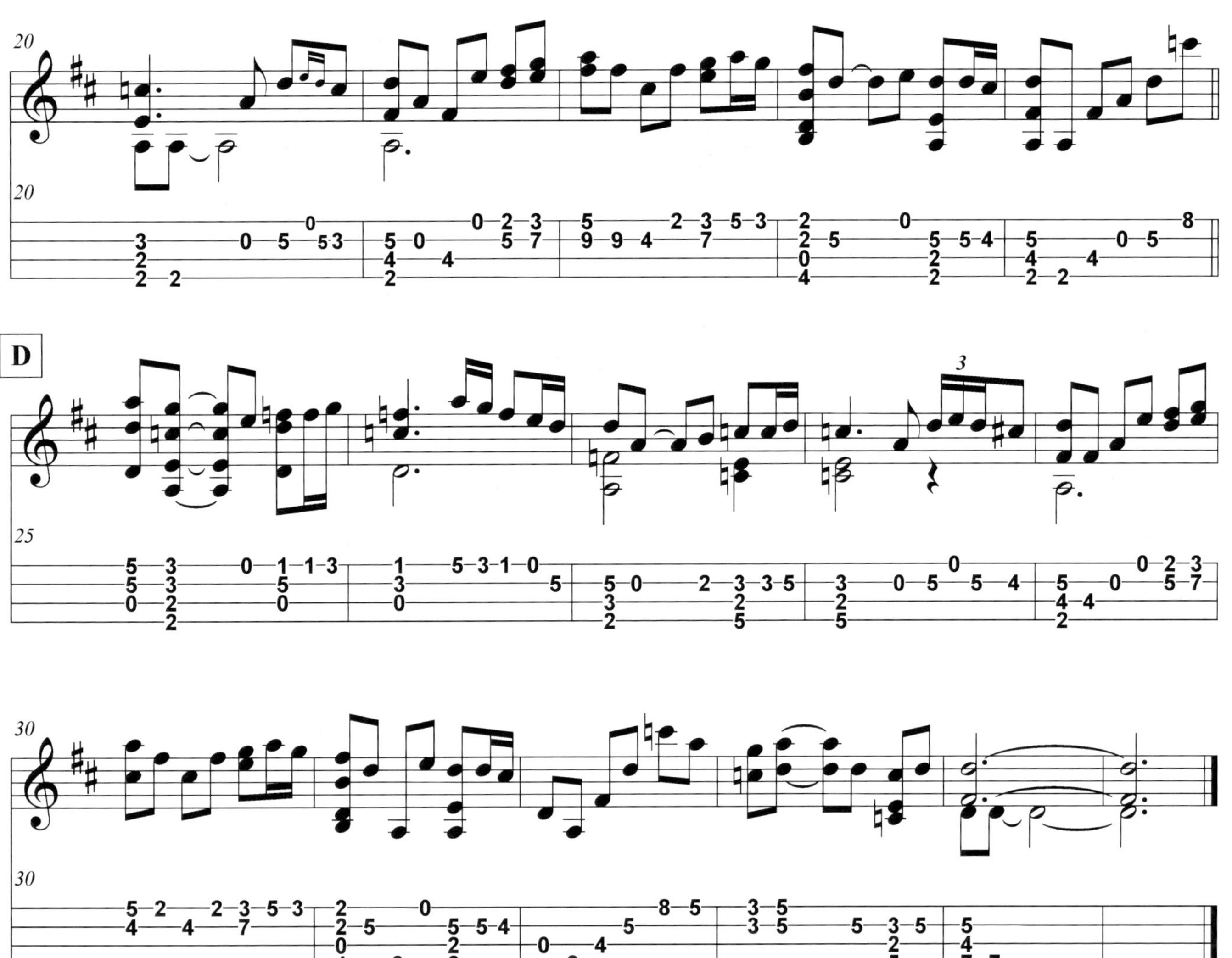
D

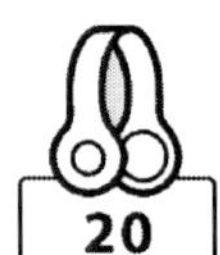

The Nativity

Rorate

Moderately ♩ = 75

Traditional Scottish

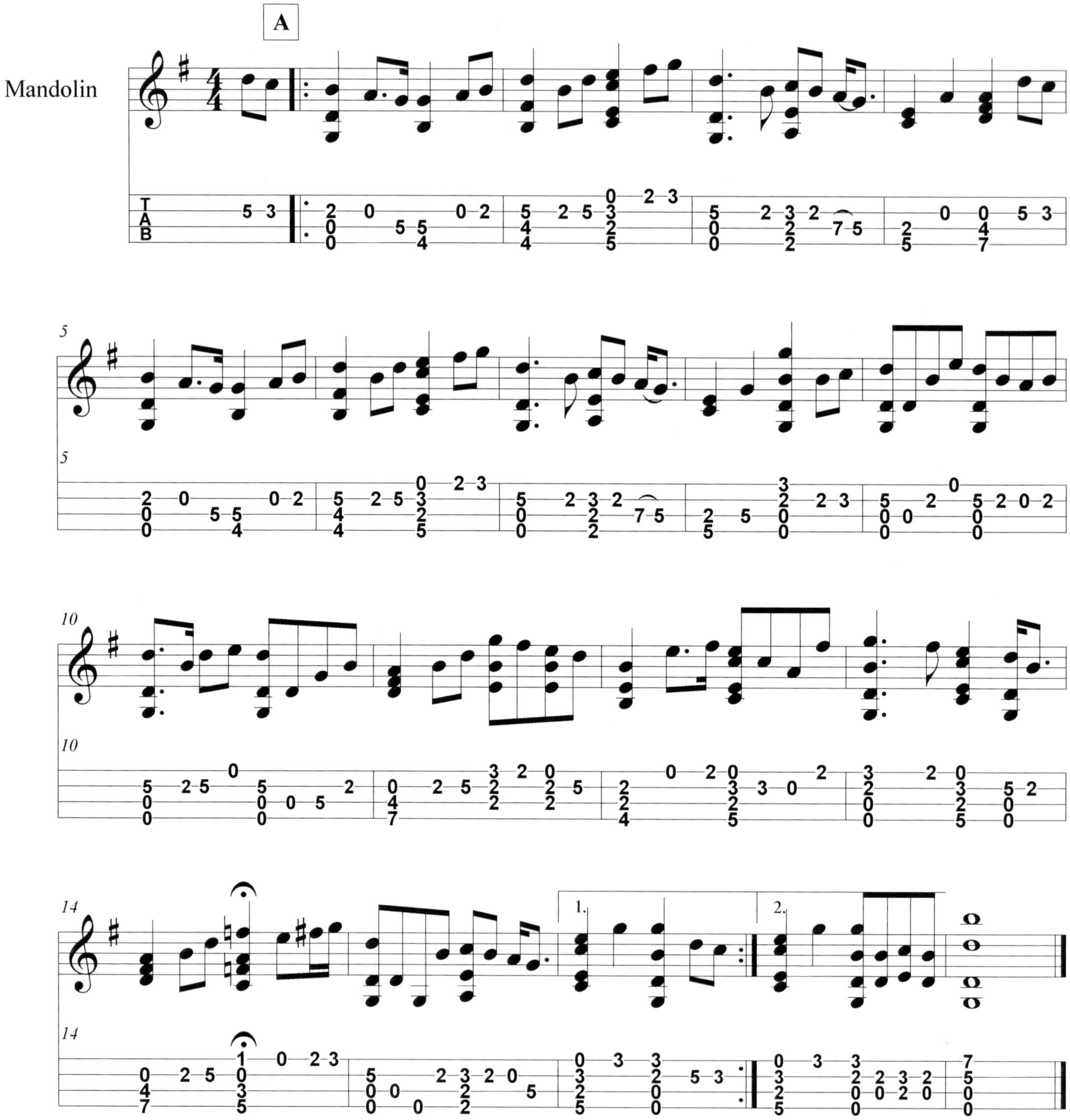

A

Mandolin